the struggle for the independence of Puerto Rico

JUAN ANTONIO CORRETJER

SECOND ENGLISH EDITION

SAN JUAN, PUERTO RICO

2020

DEDICATION

To the Puerto Rican people: To the workers and peasants; to my comrades in the struggle who found lasting life in honorable death, unforgettable losses of my troops; to the masons, tobacco workers, carpenters, painters and agricultural laborers who received me with affection and gave me their trust, friendship and appreciation with unique loyalty and unswerving faith in this new phase of struggle, I dedicate, with emotion, these pages.

J. A. C.

There is no time in the history of Borinquen when
Freedom does not protest against our colonial situation.

—*Eugenio M. de Hostos*

To begin the solution of the industrial problem:
Property for all; work for all; production and consumption for all.

—*Eugenio M. de Hostos*

Who wants to eat omelet must crack the eggs;
there is no omelet without cracked eggs or revolution without revolt.

—*Ramón Emeterio Betances*

PRESENTATION OF THE FIRST SPANISH EDITION IN 1949

With great pleasure we present to the public this work by our president, comrade Juan Antonio Corretjer. It contains, barely expanded, the concepts that he spoke of in town squares throughout the country between July and November of 1948, at the peak of the past foolish electoral campaign.

These concepts are essentially Corretjer's political thought and express his awareness and public conduct during twenty years. It is natural that now, in full maturity, those concepts gained depth and precision, enriched from many readings and experiences.

Those who have witnessed the past twenty years [1] of Puerto Rican politics will recognize in reading these pages the same impetuous and tenacious revolutionary of his earlier youth, who has learned from study and experience. And those who are young now and take on the struggle will find a true guide to the study of our political history, key to the understanding our historical processes and a manner of conduct. Because beyond the great teachings found in this book, clearly written, is the best: an exemplary revolutionary life of the author, expressed by the following words: Patriotism, lack of Self-Interest, Constance, self-possession, and manliness.

We trust that the publication of this writing will do as much good as we wish. Herein is the basic guide to our steps in the work of our organization with which we want to meet our task as Puerto Rican revolutionaries. And we hope that its study contributes to our growth and development.

Executive Committee,
UNIÓN DEL PUEBLO PRO CONSTITUYENTE

---

1 The year is 1949.

ACKNOWLEDGEMENTS: FIRST ENGLISH EDITION

The alert for the translation of this book came from Vanessa Ramos, Marta Núñez and Antonio Arturo (Tato) Rodríguez. I thank Vanessa for alerting me to what was happening regarding the change of attitude towards the independence of Puerto Rico on the part of some progressive elements in the United States; and to Marta and Tato, from Casa Corretjer, in Ciales, for telling me of the multiple requests they have received from Puerto Ricans who were born and raised in the United States, and wanted to read about the country of their ancestors and the struggles to achieve self determination and independence. Thanks to José Escoda and Vanessa for proofreading the work and making possible its completion.

The translation of this book is dedicated to all Puerto Rican Independentists who chose to endure the hell of imprisonment for a Homeland they love. We are all infinitely indebted to them for their strong spirit, courage, sacrifice and devotion.

Consuelo Corretjer Lee
October 7, 1999, New York

ACKNOWLEDGEMENTS: SECOND ENGLISH EDITION

In 1949, Juan Antonio Corretjer brought to light the political essay in book form titled La lucha por la independencia de Puerto Rico. It was an account of the colonial situation of the Island with a brief history that began with the Lares Uprising in 1868, up to 1949. The situation, as then still exists today, and with a sense of urgency, it is as poignant today as it was then. It is necessary to alert the public of the desperate need of sovereignty that Puerto Rico its islands and People face today and in the immediate future.

With deep gratitude I acknowledge and thank the encouragement and support given to the publication of this Second Edition of the translation of The Struggle for the Independence of Puerto Rico by Raúl Bernard, my husband Antonio de Jesús, Ramón Felipe Medina, María Gisela Rosado, Teresa de Hostos, and Yolanda Muñoz.

I reiterate that the translation of this book is, with great respect and admiration, dedicated to all Puerto Rican Independentists who choose to endure the struggle and even the hell of imprisonment in attaining self determination and freedom for the Homeland they love. We are all infinitely indebted to them for their strong spirit, courage, sacrifice and devotion.

In addition, we must not forget the younger generations who through their commitment will someday soon make possible Free Determination and Independence for our People and our Islands of Puerto Rico, Vieques and Culebra.

Consuelo Corretjer Lee

San Juan, Puerto Rico, November 7, 2019

FOREWORD TO THE FIRST ENGLISH EDITION

The Struggle for the Independence of Puerto Rico (*La lucha por la independencia de Puerto Rico*) was written in 1949, as an outline for historians. But more importantly, it is an eyewitness account of Puerto Rican history that has been kept out of the country's official history books. The author was a participant in the ascendancy and heyday of the *Partido Nacionalista* (Nationalist Party), and in 1936, with the rest of the party's leadership was sentenced to ten years of imprisonment and exile in a federal penitentiary in Atlanta, Georgia, and in Manhattan, New York City.

Why? Might the reader ask, is this work being translated almost fifty years after its publication? Because Puerto Rico remains a colony of the United States. Although modern technology is familiar to many islanders, and there is an appearance of economic prosperity, Puerto Ricans have no political power to decide upon economic, trade, and political policies.

The present strong push from a few politicians in Washington towards annexation of Puerto Rico to the United States, and the shift in favor of statehood of progressive organizations and individuals in that country who once supported independence for the Island, are all reasons to publish this English edition.

Statehood will mean the demise of a Latin American country that has its own cultural expressions, unique characteristics, and needs that are not consonant with the needs of the United States. The treatment of Puerto Ricans—as of native Hawaiians since the granting of statehood to that archipelago, and the Mexicans who were living in the western territories taken in the nineteenth century—will continue to be that of second class citizens dispossessed of their national identity and sovereignty.

For the United States, Puerto Rico is primarily a military bastion from which to threaten the integrity of the rest of Latin America and a source of cannon fodder in times of war.

The footnotes—not in the original text—are brief clarifications for readers who know nothing about the history of Puerto Rico. Some wordings have been changed to actualize, and to call attention to the fact that the passage of time has seen no fundamental difference in the relationship between Puerto Rico and the United States.

The names of the political parties were left in Spanish, to avoid confusion with similar names of parties in the United States.

In addition, the reader must bear in mind that America is all of the Americas, and not exclusively the portion in North America occupied by the United States.

Consuelo Corretjer Lee

December 7, 1999

New York

FOREWORD TO THE SECOND ENGLISH EDITION

The imposition by the United States Congress of a *Junta de Control Fiscal* (Fiscal Supervision Board), the push from the present pro annexation governing party, the *Partido Nuevo Progresista*, towards statehood for Puerto Rico; the scandalous behavior of that party's leaders who detoured aid for the needy following hurricanes Irma and María, as they sold favors for millionaire contracts while obeying the demands from the *Junta* to apply neoliberal austerity measures in order to pay an odious and illegal debt to *fondos buitres* from Wall Street, while unemployment and poverty rise, and many take flight to uncertainty in the United States, makes this book a necessity for those who wish for a different fate for Puerto Rico and its People.

People from the Puerto Rican Diaspora responded to the need after the two meteorological disasters by bringing food, clothing, money, water to relatives and strangers, while the governments of Puerto Rico and the United States displayed great meanness and disdain towards the plight of people in the Island.

Statehood will mean the demise of a Latin American country that has its own cultural expressions, unique characteristics, and needs that are not consonant with the needs of the United States. The treatment of Puerto Ricans—as of native Hawaiians and Alaskans since the granting of statehood, and the Mexicans who were living in the western territories taken in the nineteenth century—will continue to be that of second class citizens dispossessed of their national identity and sovereignty.

For the United States, Puerto Rico is still a source of cannon fodder in times of war. It is also an object of exploitation in terms of its natural and human resources. There are powerful extractivist interests in our mineral land resources that, if exploited, will destroy the Island as an apt place for human life.

Now, as before, *La Lucha por la independencia de Puerto Rico* is a reminder of the history of modern colonialism in the Island and provides a blueprint for self-determination and independence.

Consuelo Corretjer Lee

November 7, 2019

San Juan, Puerto Rico

CONTENTS

1

THE PEOPLE CREATE THE NATION

Despite its hardship-ridden history, its laborious and tough process of integration, its consistent efforts for expression, the people of Puerto Rico never failed itself. Whenever the need to take a step forward has called upon its strength, it has responded favorably, and the step has been taken or been attempted. If at times it has halted, if occasionally it has taken false steps, it is not to blame. The responsibility lays on those who have not obeyed the true will of the Puerto Ricans. If we examine our history, we will learn that our people have been repeatedly deceived and betrayed.

The assertion of some intellectuals and political leaders that the Puerto Ricans have betrayed their own independence and its justice is a lie. The country's history shows that, on the contrary, when called upon for historical change, the decision has always been to respond in favor. Unfortunately, the same cannot be said of the leadership. The history of Puerto Rico's steps backward is the history of its leaders. There is no history of treason on the part of the people of Puerto Rico. Historically, the people have moved forward in spite of the leaders, and they have been dead stopped by them.

It is not necessary to point out the exceptions. If there had not been any, we would not be a nation. And after the revolutionary act that took place at Lares, [2] no one can deny the existence of the Puerto Rican nation. What happened in Lares itself supports our thesis. At that time, it was not the teacher, the initiator, the encourager, the counselor, the enlightened, nor the paramount leader that failed. It was the general leadership who failed, by turning their backs on a people who had decided to be free, by impeding Betances' [3] return to Puerto Rican soil, and not

---

2 Uprising against Spanish rule that took place in the town of Lares on September 23, 1868.
3 Ramón Emeterio Betances, intellectual author of the Lares Uprising of 1868.

supporting the efforts to gain liberty. Contrary to what is generally believed, rebellions like the one at Lares have taken place many times in our history.

It is, therefore, necessary and urgent that the people of Puerto Rico think seriously about Lares, because it is the cornerstone of our foundation, the soul of our history, our life and immortality, and the life giving element to the course of our history. It is our only alternative for redemption and triumph. And it is in such a way that Puerto Ricans can do good for themselves, only to the extent that they address the issue and act through a deep and clear understanding of the fact that the Nation moves ahead in time. What inspired Nineteenth century nationalism is not a sufficient trigger to produce a Lares without defeat, nor its organizational forms enough to attain the independence of Puerto Rico.

I have mentioned the inspiration and the ways of organizing. I am not referring to the ideals of nationhood. Today, the ideals of the Puerto Rican people are basically the same as the ones conceived before the nation's birth at Lares. The process that followed has served to assess them and to refine them, and, above all, to intensify them. Not having the sovereign power to organize on the basis of those ideals, it suffers oppression and despotism, but has developed the resistance to strengthen them.

This reference to the ideals of our nationhood is unavoidable, and it is necessary to focus on our basic problem. These ideals contain the word that shakes us to the roots of our beings: Independence. If nationhood had no ideals, there would not have been an impulse towards independence; there would not have been a nation. As an object of history, independence is the capacity to realize our ideals. If we want independence, that wish does no more than synthesize into one single political formula our wish to see our ideals come true as a human group, and as a nation. This means that we want to manage, in our own way, all of the magnificent and glorious complexities that make up our spiritual and material heritage. The world may be within us, but we belong to ourselves.

If we understand, thus, our independence, then we can explain why Puerto Rico is not free. Many explanations and many factors come into play. Moreover, the basis of our colonialism is found when we examine the actions of our people as creators of their ideals, the relentless loyalty with which they have kept the faith, and the criminal deformation of those ideals perpetrated by the majority of their leaders, if not their open and unarguable treason. The Puerto Ricans have been forced to stop, recover energies and move onward, in spite of most of its leadership. When the ideals have been adulterated, it has been worse, because through deception, they became an illusion of those ideals, forcing them to take false steps, and move blindly in the terrible darkness of disorientation.

This work will examine that process during the last century and a half of our history in order to prove that, if Puerto Rico did not become free from Spain during the last century, it was not for lack of the necessary forces to expel Spanish domination from its territory. And that if it has not become independent from the United States in the present century it is not that it lacks the necessary will to end United States domination, but because, all along, two different and conflicting tendencies have been operating within the country. One, if it succeeds will redeem the Country; the other will be its doom. The first is mother of all Good the second is harbinger of our downfall.

They are the Revolutionary and the Reformist tendencies. The first is born from within our nationhood's soul; the second has been imported and is used as opium for our spirit. The first has given birth to our history, the second has frustrated the revolutionary process of the Nineteenth Century and sustained the abject Yankee occupation of our island. Puerto Rico has been close to achieving its ideals, to satisfying its needs, to winning independence every time that the revolutionary process has been strong. And has moved away from achieving its ideals, from satisfying its needs, and from independence, every time that reformism is strong. The Reformist Tendency, aided and abetted by two imperial powers, has served both* well. And therein lies the dramatic contradiction of our lives: in the terrible reality that each apparent reformist victory, which has gained credibility among the people, has been really a revolutionary victory, weakened by the reformists on behalf of the empire.

Reformism or revolution: that is the final decision to be made by the Puerto Rican people. We all know that there is no choice in the final decision. That it will be the triumph of Revolution over Reform. Our Revolution will defeat the foreign enemy as soon as it takes hold of the minds of our people. What keeps our nation chained to colonialism is imperialism's best weapon against us: reformism within. The way to defeat imperialism is to strengthen the revolutionary forces, to weaken reformism until it is useless, by neither practicing it nor imitating it. Reformism cannot be fought nor weakened by following its path, by voting in the colonial elections, by serving in its armed forces. The way to strengthen Revolution is by joining it, by helping to unite and consolidate its strengths into one force, oriented and combative outside of the Imperialist-Colonialist government, through non-cooperation, electoral boycott, refusal to pay taxes and serve in the United States armed forces; and the direct organization of the people's forces, into creating the Constituent Assembly.

The crisis of nationhood is created by imperialism to stimulate reformism. Revolution is the moving force originating from the people. The Puerto Rican Nation was born of revolution. Thanks to the revolutionary current, sometimes covert and at others overtly manifested, the Nation has survived the invasion by the United States.

In this book we will examine the historical facts that confirm our thesis.

In all countries of this planet, at all times, a more or less lengthy process creates conditions that lead to revolution. There is no such thing as an imported revolution. The statement: "All peoples will make their own revolution, if they want to; and if they do not want it, there will not be a revolution," is also true. All peoples reach the point where they want revolution. And when they do, they make it. Revolution is thus the culmination of a historic process. The revolutionary tendency in Puerto Rico, for the same reason, will show, with its growth, the progression of that process.

Puerto Rico was, as all American nations, formed under imperial rule. The American nations differ from the European ones in that while those of Europe were formed from the groupings of feudal states, the counties of the Americas spawned from the break in the continuity of their pre-Columbian history caused by the Discovery and Conquest, under the imperial rules of Spain, France, England and Portugal.

We have said that after the Lares Uprising, to deny the existence of a Puerto Rican nation is idiocy. Our nation had its beginnings long before Lares. The conquerors' exploitation of the mines through the work of the indigenous peoples; the Indo-Spanish war that ended at Yagüecas, the importation of Black slaves, the parceling of the land into lands protected by the Spanish Crown; the settling in Puerto Rico of poor Spaniards, the mixing of the races; all produced immediate differences of interests and psychological reactions that undoubtedly became factors for national differentiation. That was the beginning of our nationhood.

Three centuries witnessed the alchemy that produced the Nation, until the symptoms of formation began in an unmistakable manner. They were three hundred years of struggle, work and bloodshed, with uprisings by the indigenous people, slave revolts, runaway *criollos* and Spanish laborers from the settled areas, who managed to live independent and hardship-filled lives in the rugged terrain of the Island's interior. Bitterness, humiliation, rancor, vengeance and complexities shaped the land in which the secret chemistry of history fertilized hopes, aspirations, and decisions. It was the wonderful progression that shaped our national soul. And towards the end of the Eighteenth Century, the first blossoming of that national soul was realized in José Campeche, whose artistic genius gave birth to Puerto Rican painting.

2

THE REVOLUTIONARY TENDENCY

A man of humble origins—he was a mulatto—early on embodied another manifestation of our shaping as a nation. He was Captain Henríquez, who rose from slavery. His soul contained the melding of two races transformed into the Puerto Rican soul. He had within him the resistance and the discipline that came from hard work; the temperament forged by pain and the tenacious will strengthened by disobedience and mutinies. He was a sea captain. He was immensely wealthy. He owned a fleet of merchant vessels. Henríquez personified the Puerto Rican genius to take advantage, creatively, of materialities.

The following two individuals reveal an extraordinary progression of the will and ideological understanding of nationhood. One, the son of an aristocratic family from the eastern end of the country, and the other born to a working family from the West. As if, symbolically, they wanted to embrace between their origins the national whole, socially and geographically, they lifted our nationhood to new and lofty heights of expression. The first was Antonio Valero de Bernabé, and Roberto Cofresí, the second.

With Antonio Valero de Bernabé an ideology began to insert itself into the root of our embryonic revolutionary process. Our development acquired its first political conscience. Valero was the first Puerto Rican to think clearly about independence. If conditions had been as ripe as this extraordinary individual, Valero would have been our *Libertador*. This glorious, wise, unassuming deputy for Bolívar added to our revolutionary tradition a characteristic element of the Latin American independence movement: internationalism.

Valero was given by the society he sprung from—for being born an aristocrat—what he needed to develop his extraordinary personality, while Roberto Cofresí, for not being highborn was sentenced to the gallows and the ignominy of a black legend from which his name has yet to be rescued. Pirate, sea faring thief, cruel and cold-blooded murderer, are the epithets that Spanish historians gave him for posterity. The people, however, wove a golden legend of a native Robin Hood. There is only one point of coincidence between the two men: both exalt indomitable courage and seafaring skills.

Slowly, the truth about the native of Cabo Rojo had begun to emerge from under a century of darkness. Self-proclaimed as the leader of a republic's navy, Cofresí sailed under the banner of the Free Republic of Puerto Rico. A singular historical occurrence: the first republic declared at sea by the solitary uprising of that Ulysses of the Puerto Rican soul!

Roberto Cofresí was the first historical figure to warn us of the threat posed by the United States. No one noticed that significant and premature warning, as it was the Yankee fleet in the Caribbean, commanded by Porter that captured Cofresí and handed him over to the Spanish executioners. The United States placed its fleet at the service of Spain to thwart the independence of Puerto Rico and Cuba.

Cofresí and Marshal Valero represent the elevation of the patriotic will to heroic levels. They signify the capability of the Puerto Rican genius to command the national spirit militarily.

By the time this happened, we had already entered into the first quarter of the Nineteenth Century. That period was witness to many manifestations of Puerto Rican consciousness.

Fifteen years before, a royal commissioner landed on our shores. He was instructed by the Spanish Crown to direct from San Juan the imperial campaign against the freedom fighters of Venezuela. The presumptuous man cooked up the bad idea of including Puerto Rican militia in the invading army to our sister nation. It was enough for the rumor regarding his intentions to spread, and the now famous poster, [4] putting him on notice, appeared which said that the Puerto Rican people "will never allow that a single militiaman shall be taken to fight against our brothers from Caracas." The situation became so tense that the royal commissioner was forced to desist and even set free three Venezuelan deputies that were imprisoned in El Morro. The people were already part of the resistance, and resisted as well in 1864 when they were ordered to fight against Santo

---

4 Poster in response to the call for Puerto Rican Militia to fight against the Venezuelan independentists.

Domingo. [5] But by then, a culminating phenomenon had already occurred. The revolutionary process did not happen spontaneously. It had ideology and direction. It had its heroes and martyrs, its Vizcarrondos and Quiñoneses. Betance was in the picture, looming like a giant, his strong and apostolic figure showing on our moral spine. He was Illuminism personified; he embodied the ideas of republicanism and democracy. He was liberal democracy personified. And here, as in the rest of America, revolutionary feeling was not the artificial and violent transplant of a foreign import. It was the birth of a class whose role was to subvert feudalism in Puerto Rico and lead the struggle for independence. The bourgeoisie was born. The country had matured. The revolutionary tendency that was born out of the people, had acquired its most powerful weapon: ideology. The Lares Uprising took place, and with it, the irrefutable proof that our nationhood existed. The revolutionary process created the nation.

---

5 Santo Domingo is the capital of the Dominican Republic.

3

THE REFORMIST TENDENCY

If Revolution comes to us from the beginning of our historical lives and we take in alien elements, change their substance and make them our own and part of ourselves, it is thus the creator of our being as a people and of our living and militant consciousness.

Reform is alien, and therefore imported into Puerto Rico by two empires, fostered by them and employed by them to their advantage. It is poison that drains our energies, weakens our consciousness, and halts our development as a nation. It has deformed and alienated us. It is the empire's most powerful weapon, and our most dangerous enemy, because it is a Fifth Column that the empire has placed in our minds.

It is persuasive because it is disguised as common sense. It degenerates us because it stimulates our appetite for pleasures and tempts the less daring with the paradise of a timid and constrained family life. It glorifies cowardice as a virtue.

To be realistic is equivalent to acquiesce to abject conditions. Employing the noblest words, Reform covers up the worst of intentions. Right now it is at the peak of its degenerating effect. It has not always been like this, nor has it before been as perverse in form, personality and expression as it is now. [6] The present situation is the result of a process. But in the past and today, its effects have been the same: to surrender, to weaken the country, to delay its progress, to serve foreign rulers and prevent independence. A century of existence can lead only to the expectation of failure; but it has been useful to the empire, because it is postponing the organization of our Republic, and prolonging the pain of colonialism.

Contrary to the revolutionary tendency—which emerges from our lives and from our problems, is impelled by our will and by the

---

6 The time is 1949.

enlightenment of our thoughts—reformism is born of the policies of the ruling power. Today the United States; yesterday, Spain.

The fundamental characteristic of the foreignness of reformism is that the morally weak reformist is always willing to accept and preach the empire's slogans. That characteristic reveals its origins for it is evident that the tendency does not come from within us. It does not originate from our needs that it cannot meet. Its origin is the need of the empire to enslave and rule. Let us begin with the first noticeable manifestation of the reformist tendency. Then, it was known as assimilationism.

Pedro Gerónimo Goyco was its leader, and the political party he founded was called the Liberal Reformist Party. The first point in the party's program declared the following: "Recognize the convenience of the treatment and resolution with a liberal view, in light of the principles proclaimed by the September revolution, regarding all of the public administration, management of the economy, and social reforms of this island." [7] The second point adds: "Recognize the principle of assimilation with the Mother Country; complete assimilation, by extending to this island all of the articles in the Monarchic Constitution…"

These reformists accommodated to Spanish politics, and accepted the Spanish Government's slogans as they begged for reforms. They renounced their nationhood to call for the "assimilation to the politics of the Mother Land, complete assimilation…" The organizing impulse, the principles of their program, did not originate in Puerto Rico. They originated in the [Iberian] Peninsula.

The Spanish Unconditionals opposed them. Who would silence them? Perhaps the reformist forces? No. They were silenced by the Spanish Government, still fearful of the Lares Uprising of two years before. The project for municipal reforms, presented in 1870 by [Spain's] Overseas Minister, Segundo Moret, made it clear to those who were pro–Spain unconditionally that a systematic opposition to such reforms would lead to failure and loss of power. This lead them to the understanding that reform best served the interests of the empire; and was the best

---

7 Goyco refers to the September revolution in Spain and not to the September 1868 Lares Uprising in Puerto Rico.

way to keep the Puerto Rican people away from the path to freedom, independence and justice.

And, really, throughout its history, reformism has obeyed the Empire's commands. Thus, acting on its behalf to keep freedom, independence and justice from Puerto Rico. From the Partido Reformista Liberal in 1870 up to the *Partido Popular Democrático* of today. From Pedro Gerónimo Goyco to Luis Muñoz Marín.

And so from the beginning, the drama of the tragic contradiction is clear: while the Empire agrees to reforms because its domination is threatened by the revolutionaries, the reformists claim the victory as their own and gain prestige before the people, while at the same time they sell the people out and perpetuate colonialism, human suffering, foreign despotism and national frustration.

4

THE ABOLITION OF SLAVERY

Slavery in Puerto Rico meant paralysis and setback. It stagnated and delayed the natural evolution of Puerto Rican society. Slavery was terrible as a system. It was a production system that was met with resistance, and was, finally, overcome by Puerto Rican society. The abolition of slavery as a production system ended the evil that such a system engendered.

The institution of slavery brought Black people to Puerto Rico. Their arrival to our land and their incorporation to life in our country was a contributing element to the formation of our nation. In effect, was a contribution to our labor force, and, finally to our national integration.

The seed of rebellion grows from the abuse suffered by any race. Rebellion grew in the heart of the Black race from the moment it was enslaved. Its rebellion as an enslaved race became a part—in the course of transculturation—of the Puerto Rican national rebellion. That is why the abolitionist process [in Puerto Rico] cannot be separated from the revolutionary process. Because it was a historical revolutionary process of the nineteenth century, the mark made by slavery and the abolitionist process—although now distorted [by those who have written our history]—must have produced other repercussions that were necessarily felt in the subsequent history of the country.

Undoubtedly, however, the abolition of slavery, finally achieved in 1873, is one of the great events of our history. Without argument it constitutes a great conquest by the people of Puerto Rico in the nineteenth century. I emphasize conquest by our people and not concession granted by the colonial power.

Unfortunately, a false and pernicious romantic legend has been woven around the abolition, that reformism has nurtured and that was nurtured as well by one of the most sensitive, delicate, intense and beloved souls of our nation, [the poet] José Gautier Benítez who wrote:

"... And I bless you moved with tenderness
because only in your hospitable soil,
sweetly influenced by your external world
redemption was achieved without calvary. "

Notwithstanding the poet's words, such is not the truth. The freedom
of the Black slaves was earned with blood from the Puerto Rican revolutionaries. That calvary took place in the plains of the Toa Valley. Its
crowning glory of redemption was Lares, and it took three hundred years
to accomplish.

In order to fully understand the abolitionist process, to see how the
struggle for the abolition of slavery cannot be understood if it is arbitrarily
separated from the revolutionary process, it is necessary to destroy, first,
a lie that has been allowed to flourish harbored by ignorance and bad
faith. This lie is the assertion that in Puerto Rico slavery began with the
importation of Africans. Slavery was established by the Spanish conquerors when they took possession of the island on behalf of the Spanish King
and Queen, immediately reducing the natives to slavery in the mines and
the lands granted to the newly arrived masters by the Spanish Crown.

Before the Spanish conquerors took possession of our island and
declared it a colony of Spain, the Borincanos [8] did not possess machines,
a transportation system, electricity, aqueducts, sewers, and the indoor
plumbing we have today. Instead, they had a social organization that did
not need merchants, money lenders, bankers, landlords, prostitutes, jails,
penitentiaries, police, exploited workers, landless peasants. The natives
of Boriquén lived under a primitive communism.

The slavery régime imposed by the Spaniards upon the natives was
totally different. It subjected them to domination, destroyed their reli-
gious beliefs, and changed their customs and their social organization.
The land ceased to belong to the collective and became the private property of the conquerors, who became overnight owners of enormous
landed estates. The natives, decimated by war, forced labor, and disease

---

8 The *Taínos* were the inhabitants of *Boriquén*, now Puerto Rico, when the Spanish
    conquerors arrived.

meant enormous losses in production for the conquerors. Then, the Spaniards decided to hold on to their system by importing Africans. It was therefore the colonization that established slavery in Puerto Rico, first, by enslaving the natives and, immediately after, the Blacks.

If, as we have said, the formation of our nationhood began right then and there, and it was the revolutionary tendency, which impregnated the belly of the society that gave birth to the nation, it is noteworthy that the abolitionist process was part of the revolutionary process, a stage in the Puerto Rican Revolution. [Eugenio María de] Hostos [9] summarized that unfinished truth thus: "There is not a single page in the history of Borinquen that does not cry out against our lives as a colonized people."

A close scrutiny of the development of Puerto Rico's slave society renders historical experience that confirms yet another of Hostos' observations. "Revolutionary is and should be," he wrote, "[someone] who knows that revolution is the perennial state of societies, cannot avoid the forward move without the necessary inclination toward the ideas that must be realized; a revolutionary in the Antilles, [is] forcibly stationary and by force susceptible to move."

Hostos' description is true because the slave régime that was instituted in Puerto Rico was not identical to other slave societies in other parts of the planet. Its particular characteristics were derived from the fact that when the Spaniards took over Boriquén, Spain had a fully developed feudal state, which remained even when—first in England, France, and the United States, and then in most of Europe—capitalism was developing and eventually took hold. With the imposition of slavery on the Island, Spain imposed feudal institutions at the same time that Puerto Rico's economic development—with world conditions being what they were then—was exhibiting many elements of capitalism. This multiplicity of factors gave a strange complexity to the characteristics of the régime that governed Puerto Rico then, and complicated even more the contradictions inherent within that slave society. Because of the intelligent investment in our labor, Puerto Rico was no longer the fallow land

---

9 Eugenio María de Hostos, Independentist, Abolitionist, Philosopher, Essayist, Educator.

without direction as described by O'Reilly in his famous *Memoria*. [10] Hostos was right. Puerto Rico, forcibly stagnant by the imposed colonial situation, was by force inclined to move by the irrepressible push of the nation it carried within.

This economic, political, and social combination served to ignite the revolutionary process that, although diverse in its sporadic manifestations, was essentially due to the formation of nationhood in the Island and in line with a revolution for independence.

That is why the abolition of slavery was a revolutionary conquest by the people, and not a concession given by the Spanish Crown to the weak efforts and the hypocritical tears shed by mean spirited reformists.

In fact, the abolition of slavery in Puerto Rico was won with armed struggle. It is a truth that cannot be rationally or historically denied. Colonial historians of the reformist persuasion have distorted it in order to subvert the truth. But that denial of the truth in no way clouds the heart rending civic consciousness and dedication that led the Puerto Rican abolitionists to such a stance that their radicalism made the Cuban abolitionists shake in their boots at the Spanish Courts. Contrary to the much-praised tale of generosity on the part of the slave owners in Puerto Rico, the abolition was really the culmination of a revolutionary process. It was the graceful and well aimed gesture of a growing agrarian and landholding bourgeoisie that assumed a revolutionary stance.

But such an altruistic gesture—as expressed by the theories of the petit bourgeois intellectuals, and practiced in reality by the landlords— happens frequently, very frequently, after the fighters with weapons—the incendiary torch, the knife and the machete—wrote with blood and fire the Blacks' protests and their right to civil liberty.

It is not the purpose of this writing to list in detail the vicissitudes and progress of that struggle. It aims only to clarify our thinking about history, and to spur our memory as a people. And, perhaps, as a hint to a writer with less occupations than I, to write about in detail in a documented history of our beautiful nineteenth century.

---

10 Alejandro O'Reilly, Spanish Crown envoy who wrote a report about the state of affairs of the population in Puerto Rico during the eighteenth century.

The cornerstone of freedom for the Black slaves was their own unhappiness with slavery, manifested in two distinct ways, both of them revolutionary. The first was mutiny. Frequent uprisings by Black slaves disturbed the false tranquility of the colony. Even in 1821, one of these mutinies produced general governmental fright. It was an uprising planned in the plantations in Bayamón, that turned the fertile valley of the Toa River into the center of the struggle. The conspiracy was discovered and suppressed fiercely. The flame of insurrection brought about another attempt of rebellion in Guayama. So serious it was that the Captain General traveled to that town, leading a very large amount of soldiers. "And with great diligence—wrote Brau [the Historian]— [11] the leaders were executed by firing squad while the other slaves watched…" These uprisings and insurrectional attempts happened throughout the time that Black slavery lasted.

The other mode of expression of the Blacks' initiative towards their own freedom brought about another event of revolutionary origin: the organization of trade guilds. They were the true precursors of the labor unions. The revolutionary heart of this process is undeniable, not even by covering it with the horrendous distortions created by reformism in our labor movement. It was through those guides that the Blacks became participants in the country's leadership.

But the best evidence of how the abolition of slavery was a result of revolutionaries, were Betances and the Lares Revolution. With true political genius, Betances understood at once that the revolutionary background of the abolitionist struggle necessitated the proclamation of independence, without a doubt, in order to do away with slavery. He also understood that the revolution for independence could not take place without the participation of the Blacks. This explains the sociology of the Lares Uprising.

Betances embraced abolitionism with this in mind and used it to guide his behavior. He clearly understood that the organizing movement needed to be public and clandestine simultaneously. The abolitionist platform was used to agitate and organize publicly. The secret societies took charge of separatism. The revolution was on its way.

---

11 Salvador Brau, *Historia de Puerto Rico*, D. Appleton, New York, 1904.

And the Revolution in Lares decided the future of Black slavery. The Provisional Government of Lares decreed the freedom of the Blacks on September 23, 1868. And the following day, after The Crown defeated the Government of the Republic at the battle of El Pepino, [12] even before the interrogation of the prisoners was concluded and the process was finished, in order to take away the political clout of the Puerto Rican Revolution, twenty two days after the abolition of slavery had been decreed by the revolutionaries, on October 15, 1868, the Empire decreed "freedom to the children of slaves born after September 17, 1868." And two years later, on June 4, 1870, a law freed all slaves belonging to the state; those older that 60 years of age; those who had served under the Spanish flag; all who had not been registered in the census of December 31, 1869, and finally, it abolished slavery altogether in Puerto Rico on March 22, 1873.

The cowardice of the reformists and their political collaboration gave the Empire the ability to stop the Revolutionaries at El Pepino, and delay freedom for the slaves for five more years. What the Revolution accomplished in one day, reform took five years, waiting for the Empire to give it. And it took five years because of the threat posed by the Lares Revolution. The Revolution is the people's tool. Reformism is the brake imposed by the oppressor to deny the people's rights.

Thus, through the weakening of the revolutionary tendency the reformists—supported by the Empire—aided in the survival of psychological elements of slavery among the Blacks in Puerto Rico. They were reinfected with slavery by the Puerto Rican white reformists. It worked so well that at the beginning of the twentieth century; the Blacks collaborated with the United States invaders to form a party that promoted annexation of the Island to the United States.

If the revolt at Lares had triumphed, or if least the revolutionary tendency had remained strong, the Blacks would have been imbued by it more than any other segment of the population, and they would have been, as in Cuba, part of the vanguard in the struggle for independence.

---

12 San Sebastián del Pepino, municipality next to Lares, where the Revolutionaries lost the military fight for the Republic of Puerto Rico on September 24, 1868.

5

AUTONOMISM

If the abolition of slavery in the nineteenth century represents the great conquest of the Puerto Rican people, the autonomy of 1897 is the prize jewel of reformism. The autonomy served the Empire and thwarted independence in the late nineteenth century. With autonomy as password, calling it by different names but yet identical in reformist nature, today, reformism serves imperialism in the most efficient way by keeping the truth from the people as to what is the true common good, curtailing the path towards independence and criminally maiming the social justice they duly deserve.

As all of the reform's slogans, autonomy was born and developed to serve the needs of the Empire. Its mission is to serve it. Its goal is to be a detour to move the people away from independence.

Philip II reigned in Spain when his subjects within the territory known today as Belgium were threatening to take advantage of the empire's predicament [13] and declare independence. They were intercepted by Philip's Royal Decree, in which autonomy was granted to that territory.

That royal decree was innovative jurisprudence. The Belgians gained almost entire governance of their internal affairs and were at the same time attached to the Empire. The concept of autonomy was therefore not born out of the needs of an enslaved people, but out of the need of the Empire to dominate.

In the nineteenth century, South America was up in arms against Spanish rule, Bolívar had triumphed and the creative impulse of 1810 [14] was unequivocally felt in Puerto Rico. The thought of independence from Spain had occurred to some Puerto Ricans. Bolívar himself planned a

---

13 Spain had lost its continental American colonies and was at war with Cuba.
14 1810 marked the beginning of the war of independence from Spain of the South American colonies.

liberating expedition to Puerto Rico and Cuba. Antonio Valero de Bernabé, a Puerto Rican who was close to Bolívar should have commanded the future Liberating Army of the Antilles.

Since the United States became a republic, the most sagacious Spaniard of the time, the Count of Aranda, predicted to the Crown the [possibility of] independence of its American colonies. He devised a plan to thwart independence through the reorganization of the Empire. The Minister of the Crown, Floridablanca, was very agreeable to the clearly autonomist project. The concept of autonomy thus appears in America, not as the fulfillment of the need for freedom of our peoples, but as a need of the colonial power to hold on to its Empire.

A group of anti-independentists from Venezuela settled in Puerto Rico during the first quarter of the nineteenth century. They were aristocrats who had been ruined because of their betrayal of the cause for independence. They were highly educated people who—according to the judgment of our historians—benefitted our cultural life. We would have been better off if they had stayed in Venezuela at the mercy of the Trujillo Decree! [15] They brought to our country the notion of autonomy. If the continent were lost, autonomy would help the empire hold on to the Antilles! And that is how they thought. The autonomic notion landed in Puerto Rico, not as a benefit to Puerto Ricans but to favor imperial domination.

The setback suffered by the revolutionary forces in El Pepino, the abolition of slavery in 1873, the reform project supported by Moret in Spain in 1870, the forced exile of Betances and other leaders who advocated separatism, Ruiz Belvis's [16] death; the collapse of the revolution in Cuba at El Zanjón in 1878; the support lent to Spain by the United States so that the latter could continue its stronghold in the Antilles; all contributed to weakening the revolutionary forces in Puerto Rico and strengthened reform. The reformists thought that the time had come to concentrate their strength and eliminate the independence movement with an open push towards autonomy. And so it happened that the

---

15 Reference to Simón Bolívar's Decree of War Until Death of 1813, which vowed
      to fight until the last soldier standing, in order to gain independence from
      Spain; and defined as traitors those who did not favor separation from Spain.
16 Segundo Ruiz Belvis–planned the Lares Uprising with Betances.

Autonomist Party was organized in Ponce under the leadership or Román Baldorioty de Castro, in 1887.

However, in spite of the weakened condition of the empire, the time was not ripe for autonomic rule, because there was then no threat of loss at the hands of the independentist forces. Why should the empire agree to autonomy for Puerto Rico when it would not require a great effort to maintain the status quo? This is why the repressive *Componte*, [17] until now attributed by the reformists to the "innate cruelty" of the Spaniards endured. It was not "innate cruelty". There were reasons of state, political motives.

Repression of the autonomists did not last long. The reformists, with their usual political duplicity, have rushed to explain El Componte as despotic mindlessness and criminal insidiousness on the part of the unconditionals to Spain, and in particular to General Palacios and the Count of Santurce. Contrite for having fallen out of grace from the Empire, they rushed to ingratiate themselves with the colonial power by attributing personal and local motives to what was, in truth, motivated by imperial policy. And, with typical reformist duplicity they turned separatism into a scapegoat, reaffirming the meanness of their loyalty to the Spanish Crown and redoubled their insults to the revolutionaries. But the historical truth is that who released them from repression, who opened [the dungeons of El Morro for them to go free was Betances, the chief of the Revolution.

The sublime old man understood that the persecution against the autonomists was a recruitment source for the revolutionaries. The *palillos*, [18] the Civil Guard's sword, [Governor] Palacios's arrogance, were encouragement for discontent, and were adding to the fire of Revolution. Betances planned his immediate return to Puerto Rico, to enter the island "on foot" wielding a machete and a gun. And he hurried to contact his dear friend, the glorious veteran of the Cuban Liberation Army—exiled with honor in Central America—the Dominican Máximo Gómez, who responded with the Antillean greatness of his heroic soul; as he had always responded to Cuba's call, as he had always responded to Puerto Rico:

---

17 *El Componte,* a repressive edict emitted by Spain, that sanctioned torture of independentists.

18 *Palillos* were thin sticks of wood inserted under the fingernails as torture.

putting his sword at the service of the Antillean Revolution. The preparations of the expedition for freedom were quickly made. The hopeful fires of liberty were renewed.

Betances' contacts arrived to the island almost simultaneously with the communication from Spain that there was a plan for liberation. Alarmed, the government then lent a sympathetic ear to the autonomists, recalled Palacios to Madrid, released the autonomists from prison and allowed the activities of the Reformist Party, which refused to join Betances, reaffirmed its loyalty to the Crown, and frustrated the juncture for independence. Again, the autonomists fulfilled their servile role to the needs of the Empire, and denied freedom to the people of Puerto Rico.

As the revolutionary tendency weakened again, the Empire recovered fully its initiative to maintain the status quo. Intermittently, it blocked the autonomist movement. Baldorioty de Castro died and the movement stagnated. The party was divided, plagued by individual rivalries, struggles due to personal idiosyncrasies and political divisions. The monster of reformism showed its two heads: servility, and greater abjectness. One struggled for scraps of autonomy, the second for lesser scraps than the first. Luis Muñoz Rivera headed the second. As decadence progressed—in the long run—he predominated over the first faction as leader of the reform movement.

Nevertheless, the Antillean revolutionary movement revived and gave rise to the secret labors of Cubans and Puerto Ricans to get rid of the Spanish yoke. The Antillean Revolution had a new leader, his political genius was able to foresee the future, his energetic leadership, unheard of before in the history of America, his incomparable eloquence, and the tenderness of a father figure to all, he revived the will to fight for freedom, agglutinated the scattered efforts, and gave new shape and content to the Revolution of the Antilles. He was the Cuban José Martí. His comrade in the struggle was the oldest, most persistent and apostolic of the great workers for Puerto Rican Independence: Ramón Emeterio Betances.

No previous movement had represented so faithfully the needs, the ideals of Puerto Rico and Cuba as the one lead by Martí and Betances that was organized within the Partido Revolucionario Cubano–Sección de Puerto Rico (Cuban Revolutionary Party–Puerto Rico Section). And none had so many chances to succeed. Two enemies became obstacles to their success: two powerful allies of the Spanish Empire. They were the autonomist reform, which hovered intensely over the Puerto Ricans, and the Government of the United States. The first favored Spanish rule and served as a pacifier of the Puerto Ricans. The second employed every resource it possessed to break the links between Puerto Rico and the Cuban and Puerto Rican revolutionaries, in order to prevent revolution from igniting within our soil. That way, the Island could be taken by surprise when the United States declared war against Spain, and thus, invade and take over the nation of Betances. Martí's death at Dos Ríos, Maceo's fall at Punta Brava, Betances' poor health and advanced age—he was in his 80's—were terrible blows to the Revolution, but did not stop its forward movement.

War raged in Cuba and would also burn in Puerto Rico. Inside the rectangle that limits the beloved country, revolutionary fervor was high. The premonition of secrecy in organizing the revolutionary underground was felt. Outside both islands, the émigrés work ceaselessly to train troops, purchase arms, and to obtain funding for their endeavor. The Mayagüez native, General Juan Ríus Rivera, many times victorious over the Spanish in battle, heads the Liberating Army. There were almost half a million pesos available for the project. In the neighboring peninsula of Samaná the advance guard of the liberation forces were ready to go. One of the participants in the Lares Uprising, Aurelio Méndez Martínez, was in command there, and from there, lead the preparations within Puerto Rico. In a letter dated May 11, 1896, from Samaná, Dominican Republic, he patiently and in great detail informed the Puerto Rican underground about the organization for the uprising.

The reformists would play a last act as supporters of the Spanish Empire in Puerto Rico. Muñoz Rivera played the starring role in that orgy of political fraud. He had weakened his party to political beggarliness, to the point where it was then asking for paltry concessions of autonomy for the Island. And he strengthened his party barely enough to use the threat of revolution as a bill of exchange payable by Madrid.

Antonio Mattey Lluberas, a native of Yauco, informed Muñoz Rivera of the contents of Méndez Martínez's letter. Muñoz Rivera wrote about this in his journal: [19]

"As things were, I used to visit Yauco frequently and call on Antonio Mattey Lluberas, where Matienzo lived temporarily."

"Mattey is one of, perhaps, the most important and energetic of the few conspirators against Spain that I had met in Puerto Rico. He had sharp intelligence, strong character and will, and strong resolve. He also had connections within and without the country, great prestige among the populace, was enormously enthusiastic about gaining independence through armed struggle; and so he was a good sort of revolutionary for his persistence, diligence and great belief in his generous ideals."

"Around Mattey's dinner table, as we drank champagne, he always spoke, openly, of his purpose and means. To his own accounts—which I did not delve into nor analyzed in depth—disembarkings in Salinas, Fajardo, Guánica or Cabo Rojo, aside from being easy, were expected any time. Then, and even more in detail during our evening strolls, he talked of the pilots who knew well the coastal waters, and who would facilitate access to the Island. [He spoke] of the arms that had been purchased, and of the men who were in New York and Santo Domingo, ready for combat."

"Remember, it is June and July of 1896. Despite the tight vigilance of the secret police and the Civil Guard, several of the patriot's agents who were working [for independence] in North and South America were moving within the island."

Muñoz Rivera knew very well the value of those confidences. Perhaps only he knew their significance so fully, because of all the reformists, he was the only one who was able to deceive the people and the revolutionary leadership, as demonstrated by Mattey's [Lluberas] trust in him. Let us see what had happened before Mattey Lluberas trusted Muñoz with the nature of the plans for independence:

"Since the appearance of 'La Democracia' in Ponce, on July 1, 1890, I began what appeared to be the most patriotic endeavor in terms of the

---

19 *Obras completas de Luis Muñoz Rivera*, Volumen III. Posthumous edition by his son, Luis Muñoz Marín, Editorial Puerto Rico, Madrid.

Puerto Rican fatherland. That is, to facilitate the perfect agreement of interests and sentiments between Spain and its American colonies. It was necessary to seek a solution to the problem of Puerto Rico…" [20]

Muñoz explains the "solution" he was after in words that ooze all the venom, the impotence, the contempt that reformist have for the populace. The following quote from his journal reveals it clearly:

"Independence—inconvenient due to our special conditions—was Utopian because our poor resources would not sustain a long and bloody struggle. Annexation to the United States, although acceptable to some inhabitants of the Island, always seemed absurd to me, (Muñoz was then such a Spaniard!) [21] because of the incompatibility between the Latin and Anglo-Saxon races, the immense language barrier, the all engulfing traits of Washington politicians, and because of our people's weakened state, which makes them so prone to being swallowed up quickly."

"Having ruled out these two options, one and only one was left: that was to establish the legal, just and legitimate dominance of the sons of the country under the Spanish flag, which could be detestable for us when looked at as embodied in the presence of the Civil Guard, the conservative chiefs, the cruel punishments, and absolute authorities. But should be dear to us if looked at through the glass of self governance, democratic laws, free press and widespread suffrage."

"How could that great work be realized? How could the influence of the unconditionals be destroyed when they held complete power? The illustrious Celis Aguilera—leader of the Assimilationist Party, had drawn the solution timidly and confusedly. (The word "autonomy" was already in the Reformist Liberal Party's program in 1870). [22] And it came to mind quickly. The Autonomist Party, by itself, lacked the means to impose its agenda. But supported by organized and powerful peninsular forces, it would be able to achieve it quickly and fully."

"We could not appeal to Cánovas' conservatives because of their backward thinking and affinities with their counterparts in the Antilles. The Republicans declared themselves incapable of restoring the republic

---

20 *Obras completas de Luis Muñoz Rivera*, Volumen III. Posthumous edition by his
      son, Luis Muñoz Marín, Editorial Puerto Rico, Madrid.
21 Author's parenthetical remarks.
22 Author's parenthetical remarks.

and governing. But we had Sagasta's liberals (Monarchists), who spoke in favor of popular governance, establishing universal suffrage and stating that they did not fear 'self-government' in what remained of the Spanish Empire. Thus, the gap that created the legend of murderous hate among brothers, between them and us, was closed." [23]

And Muñoz continues:

"In 1895 I visited Madrid for the first time. The Spanish rulers and, clearly, the party leaders did not isolate themselves in their palaces nor did they stay away from the company of others. None were so open or sincerely polite and warm. It was easy for me to reach Sagasta, Maura, Gamazo, Moret, Castelar, López Domínguez, and Martínez Campos. All lauded my intentions. In all I found kind welcome. Sagasta and Moret told me explicitly that they would support the project if I would steer the opinion of the autonomists in favor of the liberal party —that is, the political assimilationism that Goyco advocated in 1870—and that they would not hesitate in implementing, from within the Congress, the program that had been agreed upon at the Ponce meeting of 1887." [24]

This, despite the fact that Muñoz reduced to a minimum the timid program passed on that year.

His hunger for a budget and his blind ambition became evident immediately, as stated in his own words:

"The future loomed brightly: Sagasta [would be] in power, legislating in favor of autonomy and granting voting rights. With suffrage and autonomy in hand... [the autonomists would be] governing and administering public funds under their own authority and popular trust and acquiescence; and not at the pleasure of an all powerful governor."

"And the pact made with Sagasta did not [only] guarantee our turn at governing. It ensured perpetual governance by the autonomists, who, with suffrage in hand would have 100,000 votes to 10,000 [of all the other parties] and would become forever arbiters of the Island's government and administrative matters." [25]

---

23 *Obras completas de Luis Muñoz Rivera*, Volumen III. Posthumous edition by his son, Luis Muñoz Marín, Editorial Puerto Rico, Madrid.

24 Op. cit.

25 Op. cit.

But Muñoz[Rivera] had to overcome some difficulties. Time was not completely to on his side. His crony, the royalist Sagasta, was not in power. And Sagasta would have been Puerto Rico's "pacifier," the Martínez Campos of Borinquen, who would win without a fight. Muñoz's position within the party was not all too comfortable. He still had strong opposition, entrenched in the idea of autonomy with greater powers than the one Muñoz defended. He had no alternative but to wait for Sagasta's triumph, which was expected soon. Fear of revolution took care of the party's internal opposition. And we quote his explicit confession:

"The Directory is made up of Gómez Brioso, Rossy, Barbosa and Sánchez Morales, the only autonomists in San Juan. They gave in immediately and called the Caguas delegation. I missed no detail in the way things were going. And I must declare that the sudden change in Matienzo and the Directory was due to the following:

First, FEAR—that's right—fear of a personal conflicting situation for those gentlemen, which as things stood, bordered on separatist tendencies. At the first hint of rebellion in any part of the island's interior, the government would arrest THOSE MENTIONED—as written here—just as it happened in 1887." [26]

Using fear of revolution, Muñoz obtained Sagasta's promise and the submission of his enemies within his party. The great treason, the Caguas Agreement, had been consummated.

Between July and August of 1900, when the Spanish flag had long left Puerto Rico, and the United States favored his enemies, and in light of later historical events, Muñoz wrote in his journal his state of mind, then. He accounts of his meeting with Gerardo Forets in 1896. The article is meant to justify his actions to his compatriots and to himself.

Forets, with a death warrant against him, defied everything and entered the country. He had already traveled from San Juan to Fajardo and from Fajardo to Ponce, attempting to recruit the autonomists. They all had excuses and sent him to Muñoz Rivera. "If Muñoz wants to we will follow his lead," they said. And risking all, Forets went to see Muñoz. They met several times. The first meeting took place in the home of Rodríguez Cabrero in the presence of the host. Pedro Fournier was

---

26 Op.cit.

present at other meetings, and on one occasion, Fructuoso Bustamante, head of the conspiracy in Ponce, was also present.

Muñoz refused. And put Forets on hold in case the efforts of the Commission to Madrid failed. His purpose was clear: to neutralize the revolutionaries for the time being so that a quick action did not bring down his unpatriotic efforts and the bureaucratic plans of the autonomists. In addition, he tried to obtain through Fournier a letter from the *Junta Revolucionaria*, to show in Madrid as proof of his loyalty and as a precipitating factor for their agreement to the terms of autonomy. [27]

Muñoz further explained his tactic, meant to take advantage of the revolutionaries that showed the extent of his identification with the Spanish Government. He wrote:

"On July 30, 1896, Rodríguez Cabrero wrote—and gave me for publication—a letter that caused profound irritation to the Government."

"As the revolutionaries were active in Santo Domingo, it was imperative to pretend to be one of them in order to keep them under constant surveillance. To carry out this work, General [Sabás] Marín engaged the services of a Puerto Rican whose name I would like to forget. Rodríguez Cabrero found this out and passed on this knowledge in detail. Immediately, the accusation followed. I was director of the newspaper and took the responsibility for writing it."

"The Commission [to Madrid] was to sail in the ship Alfonso XII, on September 6, 1896. Muñoz and Matienzo, paid a visit to the Governor General, Sabás Marín. They are talking when… The telephone rang. An aide answered it. It was a call from the chief of police. Matienzo and I, knowing that a Damocles' sword hung over my head, listened to the general at the same time that we paid attention to the telephone conversation. Suddenly, the aide, saying or revealing nothing, wrote on a sheet of paper what was being said on the line, and gave it to the governor."

"He read it, looked at me, read again, thought a minute—which felt like an eternity— and left us alone for a short while, saying he had a command to give. Matienzo and I understood." [28]

27 Edward G. Wilson, *Political Development of Puerto Rico: Struggle for Autonomy*, 1905.

28 *Obras completas de Luis Muñoz Rivera*, Volumen III. Posthumous edition by his son, Luis Muñoz Marín, Editorial Puerto Rico, Madrid.

"That message meant incarceration for me, the suspension of the [Commission's] trip; perhaps the failure of a great initiative and a well thought out plan. We exchanged a few words as he left the room and waited. General Marín returned, and asked, 'Are you the author of a seditious article that was published in "La Democracia", regarding military espionage in Santo Domingo?' The question was like an abyss had opened before me. I expected it and replied: 'No Sir. The author is one of the paper's collaborators. This is between us, in confidence, as one gentleman to another, where there is room only for the truth. But before a court of law, before a war council, I am the author, and so I have declared it, and I take all responsibility for the consequences.' 'Will you name the author of the news?', he asked. 'You sir, are an officer of the Spanish Army. You know the rules of gentlemanly behavior. And I shall sacrifice everything, before I denounce a comrade; because as publisher of "La Democracia" until yesterday, it is my duty to take responsibility for all the unsigned articles.'" [29]

"Then, he turned to Matienzo and told him to seek Public Prosecutor Mendo de Figueroa, in haste, and tell him that for very grave reasons he should desist considering the matter."

The trip to Madrid was expedited. Muñoz Rivera carried with him several letters from the General: one for Cánovas, the President of the Council, another for the Minister of Overseas Affairs, Castellanos; and the third addressed to Sagasta. Autonomy was achieved. The Captain General of Puerto Rico had "very serious motives." [30]

On March 24, in a surprise attack, the patriot Fidel Vélez, descended from the hills of Barrio Susúa Arriba in Yauco, leading a guerrilla group. At dawn, while proclaiming "¡Viva Puerto Rico Libre!" he charged, *machete* in hand, on the Spanish garrison. The attack at Yauco failed, albeit heroically. It should have been a part of the great uprising led by Betances, organized by Méndez Martínez, commanded by Ríus Rivera. But it was weakened and abandoned by the autonomists who created the conditions that propitiated the invasion by the United States Army.

---

29 *Obras completas de Luis Muñoz Rivera*, Volumen III. Posthumous edition by his son, Luis Muñoz Marín, Editorial Puerto Rico, Madrid.

30 Op. cit.

Thus, the autonomists did not win autonomy. The Spanish crown gave it to them in exchange for their defense of Spanish rule in Puerto Rico and away from the truly independentist forces that Betances led.

Had it not been for the autonomists' intervention, with the country in arms, Puerto Rico, like Cuba, should have won its independence from Spain and the United States.

The appeasing effect of the autonomy, helped by the invasion on the part of the United States, whose excuse was that permanence of Spain on Puerto Rican soil, frustrated the natural development of the revolutionary process of the nineteenth century, for the Island. At the close of the century, Puerto Rico had to take a deep breath—having been stopped on its tracks by the treachery of the autonomist leadership—and face the twentieth century to resume the struggle for independence from a young and powerful empire which had substituted the old and disarrayed Spanish Empire. The invasion brought about a new movement for independence, with new leadership that understood the inner workings of the monster that overtook it.

Let us now lift the final curtain of the great drama, let us draw a balance as to what we lost, and all that shall be achieved, which will be conquered with independence. Because when we grab our independence from the United States we must, no more and no less, regain ourselves and gain all that we have missed. Regardless of the gravity of our tragedy, the incentive [for independence] is now stronger. If, at the conclusion of the previous century we were behind Latin America in the struggle against imperialism, now we are the spearhead of our America in that struggle. The die is cast, and we will be among the victorious on Armageddon Day.

6

THE GREAT CRISIS

In the spring of 1898 the people of Puerto Rico faced the greatest crisis of their history. The United States launched a war against Spain, the first of the empire's new era.

The Declaration of War against Spain by the United States was the logical consequence of United States' policy towards Latin America since the beginning of the nineteenth century. But at the close of that century the United States had not been able to propitiate the results that it was "patiently" preparing for almost one hundred years. Spain's proud resistance was in the way. The dream of expelling that country from the Antilles in order to control them had to be modified. So, the United States engaged Spain in war in order to force an alliance with that country in the exploitation of the Antillean wealth. The Treaty of Paris [31] is a direct consequence of this circumstantial modification in the policy of the United States, and it turned Puerto Rico into a colony of the United States. The Cubans have already assessed the meaning of this act for Cuba.

The autonomists' "victory" of 1897 meant the tragic weakening of the revolutionary forces. This was the clue to the United States' easy victory in securing its plans for Puerto Rico. The invasion of Puerto Rican soil tested the reformists' patriotism, their political capabilities, their personal courage, and ironically even their "loyalty" to Spain. They failed miserably in each and every one of them.

Driven to an unprecedented state of weakness through the isolation created by the autonomists-reformists; and by the annexationists headed by Henna who infiltrated their ranks, the revolutionaries, nevertheless, displayed patriotic dignity, national consciousness and shame. When the elderly and frail Betances received the news in exile, his response, as valid then as now, was: "I will not accept the colony, neither with Spain, nor

---

31 Treaty between the United States and Spain, after the Spanish American War ended, that turned Puerto Rico into a colony of the United States.

with the United States. What are the Puerto Ricans waiting for? Why do they not revolt?"

Betances' battle cry reached into the soul of Puerto Rico. A rebel patrol on horseback, lead by guerrilla fighter Águila [Blanca] shot at the Yankees in Guánica. Spontaneously, a rebel movement known as the Partidas Sediciosas (Separatist Troops) was formed and spread widely within the country's interior. That I know of, the enormous importance of this spontaneously formed armed movement, which in its beginnings was compelled by some serious revolutionary conspirators, has not been documented. Had the autonomists responded with political responsibility, personal courage, and patriotism, the significance of such a movement would have been of transcendental importance. But, without political support, the Partidas followed the path of every disintegrating guerrilla movement: delinquency. However, had the autonomist-reformist leadership given direction and the right political context to the guerrillas, that movement might have at least lessened the country's disgrace. For the last time in his life, Muñoz Rivera had the chance to be a patriot, but he lacked greatness. Once more, the people responded and the leadership failed.

The political ineptitude of the autonomist leaders reached its peak when the Autonomic Cabinet resigned with bowed heads. Accustomed, as they were, to obeying an imperial power, they heeded the commanding tone of the Yankees. Like lambs to the slaughter, they hurried to hand over their resignations as requested by the United States Army. Muñoz Rivera, Juan Hernández López, José Severo Quiñones, Manuel F. Rossy, Francisco Mariano Quiñones and Manuel Fernández Juncos sold out. Those same men would soon after constitute, with one more individual, the leadership for collaboration with the new master. And they served him with as much "loyalty" and efficiency as they served the former.

Having lost the opportunity for insurrection, Hostos tried to organize a political rebellion. He founded the League of Patriots, which should have been a means for national unity. The old autonomists, aghast by the ovation he received during a public meeting, boycotted his work. Even the League—with Hostos in it, maintained the liberating purpose but was really a concession to reform—frightened the former autonomists.

The journalists from the revolutionary camp wielded their pens against the invasion, while the old autonomist scurried, cowardly, to adapt their old appeasing language to the demands of the new master. While Guzmán Rodríguez was jailed, as would later be Medina González, and Evaristo Izcoa Díaz dies stoically in a Ponce jail, Muñoz Rivera, Barbosa and their kind compete for first place in the favors of the United States. Thus, the submission of the autonomist leaders validated a political base for the invaders.

Old autonomist factions, splinters from the unconditionals to Spain, and elements of the annexation persuasion that had infiltrated the Junta Revolucionaria in New York, were aligned on the new colonial political arena.

The United States realized that this servile criollo reformism would serve to keep the country pacified. So it manipulated the reformists by placing them in bureaucratic posts and cutting Puerto Rican unity to the quick. The eternal imperial motto of "Divide and conquer". Generals Miles and Schafter had been given instructions by the War Secretariat of a divisive plan that they would apply equally to Cuba and Puerto Rico. Keeping in mind that the Cubans were accustomed to defending their rights with weapons, that there were racial divisions there, and the Blacks were predominantly in favor of revolution, the United States stimulated racial prejudice and placed its resources with the white criollo aristocracy. The plan did not frustrate independence for Cuba, but it divided the Cubans and forced them into civil war.

The instructions given to General Miles, chief of the invading forces in Puerto Rico, indicated that the Puerto Ricans were not accustomed to defending their rights with the force of arms, rather they were inclined to political discord. The island's population was mostly white, and in order to attain divisiveness, racial prejudice must be encouraged. In order to do this, the Army would lend resources to the Black minority. The plan worked well in Puerto Rico. The Blacks, who learned submission from the white reformists, served to organize the Historic Republican Party—which had the unequivocal favor of the government—lead by [José Celso] Barbosa. Muñoz Rivera led the organization of the opposing *Partido Federal.*

José Celso Barbosa was extremely pro–Yankee. He was "the man" of the invading government, the unconditional annexationist. Neither he nor his followers have ever denied that fact. But the reformists from Muñoz [Rivera's] camp have gone to great lengths to cover up for their leader, and present him as a champion of liberty, and as a great strategist. But his adhesion to the new master, as soon as the Spanish flag was lowered, leaves no doubt that he was not. He assumed the same position regarding the United States that he had when Spain governed the island. Compare the two following declarations. [The first was published in the newspaper "La Democracia" in 1892, the second, from an interview with the "New York Tribune", published in October 10, 1898]:

"… It is necessary that we administer [Puerto Rico] in all of its aspects. Our propaganda is directed to achieve that end. Everyone in the country already knows that we are Spanish democrats and we go before the Spanish democracy in good faith, without pessimism or reserve…. On that basis we can enter into agreements with the peninsular groups, not with the purpose of serving them blindly, but with the purpose of obtaining complete reciprocity which will put us in the position to lead the colony…"

But a few days after the exchange of fire between Spain and the United States had ceased he said: "The general desire can be condensed in the following formula: a brief, very brief military occupation, lasting until the Congress in Washington convenes; during the military occupation, the laws and the governing bodies that now exist must be respected; later, followed by declaring [Puerto Rico] a territory with legislation that adapts to national laws, but no less autonomic and free than what we now possess. After a short while, to declare it a state, which would fulfill the wishes of all [Puerto Ricans] and would completely identify them with the new fatherland. This is the simplest and easiest method to 'americanize' Puerto Rico…"

Although the submission of the leaders was important for the Empire, it did not offer enough guarantees. How was the United States government to trust men who from one day to the next swore allegiance to two foreign sovereigns of their country? Their submission would be used to organize systematic submission of the governing class and the masses. Suffrage, which was dependent upon Yankee dominance and ruled by that foreign political power; was the great formula through which the people would waste their political energies with the assistance of the submissive leaders. And in order to decimate the liberating energies of the people, the military occupation was imposed. And to break national continuity, the economic interdependence among Puerto Ricans must be destroyed.

The material foundation of nationality is, by necessity, the economic interdependence between those who inhabit a territory. For Puerto Rico, that base was coffee. So, coffee economy had to be eliminated.

A few months after the United States flag was flying over Puerto Rican soil, the cities in the island received the first waves of hungry former coffee growers who sought shelter and would join the ranks of the first pro–Yankee candidates for posts in the colonial bureaucracy. They were the true vanguard of the bureaucratic plague that has befallen the country. The destruction of the coffee industry had been accomplished.

The former proprietors of land were not alone. After them—half of the population earned a livelihood from the coffee industry—thousands of workers who had been once employed in the processing of coffee, rushed to the cities. Just a few months after the takeover by the United States, the pestilent slums that upset us were spawned. All this was the result of the first assault of the imperialists on the economy of Puerto Rico.

I quote a publication of the United States Government, on pages 55 and 56 of the book, Puerto Rico, a Guide to the Island of Boriquén, compiled and written by the Puerto Rico Reconstruction Administration, in cooperation with the Writers' Program of the Work Projects Administration, sponsored by the Puerto Rico Department of Education, and published by The University Press Society, New York in 1940. It says:

"The use of Puerto Rican legal tender—the peso—which had been at the same rate of exchange as the coin of the United States in 1898, was abolished in 1899 and substituted by the dollar at the rate of 60 cents for every peso. This caused a readjustment of values at the Island's disadvantage, whose economy was based on the peso. At the time, coffee was the economic backbone of the island with 58 million pounds exported yearly. The coffee growers, moved by the half century of consistent demand for their product in Europe, were enjoying an abundance of production. They mortgaged their properties to purchase more lands, and the money exchange increased their debt. That was made worse by the destruction wreaked by the hurricane San Ciriaco, of that same year, which felled the coffee plantations. It was the final blow to the coffee industry in the country."

Having lost their properties, the farmers were forced to migrate to the towns and cities. Followed by the workers who were forced to raise their hovels around the urban areas, giving rise to the foul smelling slums that still exist. The ruin of the coffee industry, which employed more than half the population was nothing more than one dramatic detail in the overall ruin that the exchange of the coin brought to the country.

There is yet another fact that adds to the responsibility of the invading government for the economy's collapse. Of course, if the farmers had not seen their finances diminished by 40 percent due to the exchange; or in equal measure the agents' reserves (the ruin of commerce began with the ruin of the agents). The growers, with their own resources in addition to the credit that the agents gave them would have been able to face the crisis valiantly and victoriously. Such conditions had disappeared. But had the invader felt any responsibility towards the invaded, it would have rushed to grant reasonable credits to satisfy the immediate needs of the industry. But on the contrary, as evidenced in a maliciously revealing book of the time, published by Edmund G. Wilson, Political Development of Puerto Rico, the government not only denied the loans, it teased the growers between denial and hope, paralyzing their own initiative, contributing to the deterioration of the coffee groves with the delay and pushing the proprietor class to serve as basis for the submission of the reformist leadership. The same happened with the laborers.

On the day that the Autonomist Cabinet took office, workers walked the streets of San Juan carrying two flags: one with the single star on a [sky] blue triangle–symbol of our nationhood–and the red flag of labor. Right then and there, Muñoz Rivera revealed in practice what he had written months before: that the autonomists "would become the eternal arbiters of the Island in matters of government and administration". No opposition [would be allowed]! Much less class opposition! The workers' demonstration was disbanded. But that afternoon, at a workers' meeting held at the Municipal Theater, the speeches openly spoke in favor of independence and socialism.

There is evidence that throughout the nineteenth century the Puerto Rican bourgeoisie was developing. From the time of the founding of the Sociedad de Amigos del País (Society of Friends of the Nation) to the repression of the workers' demonstration of 1897, much had happened. From "itself a class" the bourgeoisie became a "class for itself". They were undone by the invasion.

Parallel to the development of the bourgeoisie, from the beginnings of the craftsmen's guilds, the working class was also evolving. The 1897 demonstration showed its natural growth towards the conquest of independence for the country and for its class interests. The invasion changed its course. Until the time when the workers' leadership betrayed the movement and embraced the exploiters of the people. Because in spite of what happened in 1897, by the turn of the century the working class in Puerto Rico did not have organizational nor ideological unity. Marx was known in a confused manner, barely by name. The names of Julian de Sores, Kropotkine, Pablo Iglesias, Ferrer, were mentioned without true knowledge of their endeavors. With that confusion, with the hunger caused by unemployment, and the unexpected abundance of settlers in the slums, the Empire was able to operate and lead the young workers' movement to the most vulgar form of economism, to a most pernicious reformism under a leadership transformed into a workers' aristocracy of the colonial kind.

A man, not a Puerto Rican but a Spaniard, became to the working class what Muñoz Rivera was to the bourgeoisie. He was Santiago Iglesias Pantín.

Just as the role that Muñoz Rivera could have played in gaining freedom for Puerto Rico is evidenced in these pages, as well as the role he really played in stopping that movement, the role played by Iglesias, as leader of the country's workers is also highlighted when we examine the transformation that took place during the first eighteen months of United States rule, with the new relationships between the social and political forces wrought by the invasion.

On April 12, 1900, the Congress of the United States approved the Foraker Law, establishing a civilian government in Puerto Rico. The approval of that law meant the stabilization of imperial rule. The country had been weakened enough to give an appearance of civility to the despotism of armed occupation.

Investments began with the civilian government. The country's ruin made it easy. The sugar and tobacco industries expanded, protected by tariffs. The sugar industry displaced the agrarian economy from its direct agricultural base—based on local consumption—to the commercial production for export. The production of tobacco and citrus fruit went the same route. But the coffee industry was left unprotected by the tariffs, and so it went from an industry in ruin to an unimportant one.

The imperialist plan was clear. The material support for nationhood had to be destroyed, and the wealth of the country transferred to imperial hands. The plantation mills in the sugar industry, which produced brown sugar, gave way to modern sugar mills that ground the cane harvested from thousands of acres. The family farm, developed in the course of four hundred years, disappeared, suddenly swallowed by the great absentee corporations. Eighteen months after the invasion, the end of 1900 had absorbed the 21 mills and the 249 individual plantations that existed in 1899 absorbed into 41 enormous modern mills. Absentee proprietors from New England, New York and Philadelphia, owned the country. The aggressive takeover on the part of Yankee industry over the vulnerable Puerto Rican agrarian economy had engulfed our sugar industry.

Such conditions created an explosive situation. It would have been easy to organize and lead a strong workers' movement that would also propitiate a national movement for independence, in which the workers would play an extremely important role. That importance would not have been reduced by the coincidence of great strategic force, but would also have been reflected in the thought of the national revolutionaries, expanding their progress, as did the penetration of the peasants and the tobacco workers within the spheres of the middle class in the liberating command of Cuba, represented by Martí, the Maceo family, and Carlos Baliño, determined a qualitative change in the content of the Cuban Revolution.

In Puerto Rico, that liberating movement took place. But both forces, the bourgeoisie and the proletariat, divided by the invader, took different paths. And on both paths, the first serious movement of liberation under United States domination was frustrated. Reformism again undermined its base and both currents ended up embracing the invader with servility. It is necessary to point out, however, that in spite of its failure, the significance of that movement for both camps is enormous.

7

UNIONISTS AND SOCIALISTS

The *Partido Unión de Puerto Rico* (Unity Party) was, as its name implies, an effort to meet the expressed need of the people for national unity in order to face the conditions created by the invasion. In terms of mobilization and organizational effort its success is undeniable. It failed terribly, however, in attaining its historical objective.

The Partido Unión de Puerto Rico was born when a segment of the ruling class realized the true meaning of the invasion. When intellectuals such as Rosendo Matienzo Cintrón and José de Diego realized what the country's situation really was but they did not understand the true nature of [United States] imperialism, or its essence.

Matienzo realized that the presence of the United States flag in Puerto Rico was equivalent to a surrendering Puerto Rican lands to United States' landlords. He put forth a thesis of political agrarianism. De Diego understood well that the presence of the United States flag in the Puerto Rican sky was a death sentence for the culture. He began to think seriously about the need for independence. Those two very different men were alarmed at the Empire's aggression to the economy and the culture.

Matienzo and De Diego represented the uneasiness within the bourgeoisie [with the new colonial situation]. The Partido Unión de Puerto Rico was born when the Puerto Rican bourgeoisie understood that it needed a banner to defend the lands remaining in their hands. That banner was the flag of independence. But neither De Diego nor Matienzo led the party. Ironically, Muñoz Rivera led the first independence movement of the twentieth century, and thus, its failure was practically guaranteed.

The Partido Unión de Puerto Rico was the national ruling class party. But because it basically responded to the dearest aspirations of the people, it became the party of all Puerto Ricans.

The fight for independence was the effort to save the country. The struggle to retain the lands in the hands of Puerto Ricans was, as well, the struggle for social justice. Aware of what this entailed, the people did not fail, and they overwhelmingly supported it over all others.

But as the people joined the Unity Party to carry out the necessary task [of independence], the leadership took the much trod reform route and devious path of opportunism. The party should not have gone to the polls. It should have organized armed resistance and rebellion. Instead, it was led to elections and the people followed it into frustration and disaster.

Muñoz Rivera learned from the failed Partido Federal, that in order to win elections in Puerto Rico, it was necessary to obtain Washington's previous approval. Once obtained, the competing parties are free to fight one another as viciously as they like. But they are not Puerto Rican parties competing against one another, they are factions racing to better serve the Empire in exchange for managing the budget. There are degrees, of course, but the road to the polls inevitably leads to collaboration.

It was not difficult for the Empire to deform and break up the Partido Unión de Puerto Rico. In vain, Matienzo insisted on his agrarian gospel. The sugar boom, brought by the imperialist first world war of 1914, broke the ranks of the criollo landowners and merchants. In vain, De Diego resorted to his wonderful oratory skills in defense of the language, the culture and independence. Abandoned by his own class, De Diego became a lonely conscience that did not know how to appeal to the masses. They would have supported independence and would have been enough to carry the cause to victory.

Muñoz Rivera's opportunism triumphed. He had gone completely to the annexation camp. He spoke to the masses of independence in order to gain their votes, but presented the candidacies of his party—annexationists like Martín Travieso, Juan B. Huyke, Hernández López, and others—to Washington. Under his guidance, the party ended up not saving the lands for the Puerto Rican bourgeoisie, not obtaining independence, but strengthening the absentee landowners interests and the passage of the Jones Law of 1917, which forced United States citizenship and compulsory military service. The party was led down the reformist electoral path and eventually disintegrated.

The Partido Unión de Puerto Rico was the last concerted political effort of the Puerto Rican bourgeoisie to save the country by trying to save itself. They failed because they did not recognize that their task was to lead the revolution for independence; when they became obfuscated by the sugar boom brought on by the war, and forsook what should have been its objectives: to make the country independent, to insure that the lands remained in Puerto Rican hands, and to create an internal consumer market.

That is why the only positive thing that remains of that party is the testimony that the people responded to its call. If, instead of moving forward it went backwards, it was not because of the people who, even when the party's leadership eliminated independence from its agenda as a national solution, kept calling for it. But the weight of the leadership was such that their backwardness unfortunately resulted in a generalized backward move: we lost the juridical recognition of our own [Puerto Rican] citizenship, the municipal autonomies, and the implicit recognition on the part of the United States that the country was on its way to liberation.

The unionist leadership, with the exception of De Diego and a few students and intellectuals that went to his camp, betrayed the country. The basis of the treason was reformism, because in leading the country to elections, it bound it to imperialism. In Puerto Rico, the electoral process legally binds any participating party exclusively to the legal means of struggle adding it to the reformist wave, because the need to win elections takes precedence over all other endeavors, and independence is relegated to a secondary plane. Repeatedly, history has taught us that independence will not be won through elections.

If the Partido Unión de Puerto Rico destroyed itself by resorting to divisionism and treason, the Partido Socialista, founded by Santiago Iglesias Pantín a few years after the invasion, never lived up to its name. Nothing has been more peculiar and terrible than the colonial "socialism" born and bred under the protection of Yankee Imperialism through the social-imperialist Samuel Gompers and his counterpart in Puerto Rico, Iglesias Pantín. And nothing is more tragic as well—due to the conditions of the working class—when that party was organized and detoured away from its revolutionary and patriotic core, and lead towards collaboration-ism and betrayal.

In effect, there is not a more meaningful detail that can be pointed to in order to demonstrate the historical progress of Puerto Rico during the latter half of the nineteenth century than the combativeness of the working class at the turn of the twentieth. In a previous chapter, we noted the memorable event that took place as the Autonomic Cabinet was being sworn in: The flag with the triangle and the [single] star—the symbol of nationhood—was publicly held up high for the first time, deliberately and defiantly next to the red flag. At the workers' assembly held that same day, independence and socialism were discussed openly.

The important role that the workers could have played in the eman-cipation of Puerto Rico was detoured by [Iglesias'] Partido Socialista. But that party—which the people joined as disappointment with unionism grew—was since its inception unpatriotic and without ideology in spite of the fact that it led the masses through great struggles to gain better salaries in addition to some other minimal gains. With its surrender to Imperialism the Partido Socialista gave the empire its base with the masses and was so damaging to the country that the workers' movement was broken, its immobility in the face of the present national problem (and with most of the unions supporting Imperialism) can be traced to one person: Santiago Iglesias Pantín.

The phenomenon that was Santiago Iglesias Pantín, organizer of the workers' movement and founder of the Socialist Party, cannot be simply explained by the fact that he was not Puerto Rican. Although it is true that he arrived to Puerto Rico as a mature man, he could not have had the childhood memories nor the past linking his affections to the country. But he could have overcome that had he been ideologically pro-labor. The fact is that he had always been a petit bourgeois politician and, opportunistically aligned himself with the new masters of the country.

[Iglesias] lacked the ideology that favored the workers. He did not recognize the role that the bourgeoisie could have played in the struggle for independence, nor did he recognize the importance of independence as a weapon of the proletariat. His ignorance of working class ideology prevented him from realizing that the struggle was then, as it is now, for national sovereignty as a basic conquest for the workers in their historical progress. The struggle for political independence is fundamental and must not be delayed for the economic necessity of the working class. It is the only way for it to repossess the homeland.

He imbued his lieutenants with his contempt for Puerto Rican nationhood. This was not because he was a foreigner. He could have had positive feelings toward the nationhood and appreciated its worth. But he did not understand the ideology of the working class and, opportunistically, allied himself with Social-Imperialists such as Gompers, to do his best to destroy it.

Iglesias' hatred of independence and his overt contempt for the nationhood were not born of his foreignness. They were the product of his lack of internationalism. Iglesias was never an internationalist. His Socialist Party was never part of an international movement, nor did he understand the problem of independence for Puerto Rico in relation to the general problem of capital, of overthrowing Imperialism, of the proletariat revolution. He never understood the Puerto Rican independence movement as part of the movement of the colonies toward independence in a revolutionary alliance with the workers of the imperialist countries.

Had [Iglesias Pantín] been an internationalist, he would have seized the banner of independence with a revolutionary passion greater than the most recalcitrant nationalist. He would have understood that without a nation there is no internationalism. His brand of internationalism was nothing but a vague, confused and malicious "worldism" used to detour the nascent—yet courageous and patriotic—working class movement towards most vile annexationism. If Muñoz Rivera served Imperialism by helping to detour the bourgeoisie into producing sugar to aid the war effort, Iglesias [Pantín] served it by leading labor to work for Imperialism. His fake internationalism was the prologue to the recent globalism—vague, unscientific, devoid of reality, and malicious.

[Santiago Iglesias Pantín's] most brilliant disciple of apostasy is Luis Muñoz Marín, [32] [political] offspring of Luis Muñoz Rivera and Santiago Iglesias Pantín.

---

32 Leader of the *Partido Popular Democrático* in 1949—when this book was written—and son of Luis Muñoz Rivera.

At the end of the nineteenth century, Puerto Rico's working class favored unionization. If it had followed the spontaneous process that had begun with Lares, the labor movement would have organized its own political party. The leadership would have emerged to direct the union movement, and through the struggle, the proletarization of the middle class would have brought to its ranks intellectuals that would have strengthened it. Perhaps it would have moved slowly, but sincerely and efficiently, down the historical road to battle for national liberation. It might have been the force that would have stopped the divisionism of the unionists, the force that at the decisive moment would have held a gun to the unionists' heads and forced them to go forward in the struggle for independence.

Iglesias' arrival [to the Puerto Rican political arena] curtailed the struggle for independence. Mature and experienced, it was not difficult for him to win the admiration and following of the nascent labor movement, young and ideologically unclear. With his false internationalist credo, Iglesias took away the Puerto Rican flag from the workers and exchanged it for the Yankee flag of tyranny and imperialist exploitation. Entrenched in the falsehood that the independence movement was reactionary he thrust the working class against the young Puerto Rican capitalism, and helped the Empire to dismember it and make it fearful of class struggle.

The independence movement has never been and is not reactionary. Always, organizing of our independence would be a factor in weakening imperialism, which proves that the movement for independence has always been progressive. The class struggle would not have ended because labor allied itself with the bourgeoisie in the struggle for independence. On the contrary, in fighting together with the national bourgeoisie, labor would have become stronger, conquering for itself in the struggle the gains that the Constitution of the Republic would have to grant it. With his methods Iglesias frustrated as well the formidable promise of leadership that the working class had begotten. Iglesias served (and this was his greatest service to imperialism) the imperialist tendency to pick out from within the workers with leadership qualities to create privileged categories and separate them from the rest of the masses, giving rise to a labor aristocracy.

Iglesias turned the labor movement into a typical colonial economist movement. His struggle was only for wages and his party was pro–imperialist, with the slogan of "permanent union with the United States". "Iglesism" would be a more appropriate name for his type of leadership. It plunged the movement into reformism from the start. It is true, however, that in the beginning it did not limit itself to the legal ways of struggle, but that in no way diminishes his reformist character, because his entire struggle, for labor and in his political party, were only geared to obtain reforms. In that case, the party's terrorist phase is no more than a manifestation of the economism fundamental to Iglesias' struggle. It is a known fact that labor preoccupied solely with economic gain, follows one of two paths: either gives in to power and begs for reforms, or uses terrorism. Both roads lead the followers of "Iglesism" to a total surrender to Imperialism.

And so, the final surrender through the party was openly accomplished during the 1920s when it joined the worst reactionaries and capitalist annexationists in an electoral race. The party took in the bureaucracy entering fully in the fight in favor of imperialism. Having done this, Iglesias pronounced the unforgettable: "The homeland is the refuge of scoundrels," precisely at a time when imperialism was conducting a bloody persecution of the nationalists. These words almost cost him his life and forced his flight from the country and from the hearts of the Puerto Ricans, for good.

Thus, the Puerto Rican bourgeoisie lost the last opportunity for a concerted effort to salvage the country by saving itself, and the first attempt of the working class to create its own party and through it serve its own interests and move closer to independence.

In both instances two fundamental facts stand out: first, that in the Unionist and the Socialist parties, equally, when there was the call for independence and social justice, the rank and file was in favor and the leadership was not; and second, that in each party the weakness of the revolutionary forces left the door open to reformism and betrayal.

8

ALLIANCE FOR SLAVERY

On October 21, 1929, the New York Stock Market collapsed. The world did not understand quickly enough, the breadth of that event. It should have for it was a very bitter lesson. The crash was the greatest cyclical crisis of Yankee capitalism.

But the most alert, perspicacious and knowing observers had detected the upcoming crisis. Having beforehand thrust the inevitable crisis upon its colonies and semi-colonies, the imperialists had offered them, for only the keen observers to see, the anticipation of what would be its own disaster.

Years before, Puerto Rico had its economic structure cracked when it was reduced to complete servitude. A lot can be written about the political repercussions of the crash. But it is necessary to examine first— for the sake of continuity and logic—the analysis of a political juncture that is sort of a contradictory prologue.

The *Partido Unión de Puerto Rico* did not participate in the imperialist colonial elections of 1924, because it had lost its substance, and the *Partido Socialista* was increasingly threatening the annexationist *Partido Republicano*. Both were forced into an "alliance" under the leadership of the Unionist Antonio R. Barceló and the Republican José Tous Soto.

This new formation received the name of *Alianza Puertorriqueña* (Puerto Rican Alliance), and was an attempt to erase the failure of unionism and make it seem as a triumph of unification. The Republicans had nothing to lose, because unionist support brought them out of the political exile that their nauseating pro–annexation politics had put them in. The union of both forces was an alliance to sustain colonial servitude.

Simultaneous with the formation of the Alianza in 1923, the *Partido Nacionalista de Puerto Rico* (Nationalist Party of Puerto Rico) was founded from a small splinter group of the *Partido Unión de Puerto Rico*. Another group of staunch annexationists that broke off from the *Partido*

Republicano Histórico (Historical Republican Party) founded the *Partido Republicano Puro* (Pure Republican Party), led by Rafael Martínez Nadal.

The *Imperialists both thought of the Alianza Puertorriqueña* as the destruction of the independence movement, and the elimination of the move towards annexation that the Empire had encouraged at the beginning of the occupation. *The Alianza* defended the status quo, just as the *Partido Popular Democrático* (Popular Democratic Party) is its present [33] staunchest defender.

The Empire's mistake regarding the independence movement was as great as its reasoning with respect to the "weakness" of the Puerto Rican nationhood. Instead, the formation of the Alianza was the prologue to the greatest independence movement that the country has had in this century, because the Partido Nacionalista was born from it. At the beginning, it had no influence of note in the country's events. Any party, and most of all a liberation party, is not born exclusively of the will of a group of people that associates voluntarily to give it life. It also needs the intricate and sometimes invisible network of conditions that gives it a reason for existence and historical thrust. Between 1923 and 1930, it [the party] did not recognize its leader. As Martí said: "Sometimes the man is ready, but the people are not. And when the people are ready, the man does not come forth."

The contradictions inherent to the Empire's development would highlight the horror of the emptiness of the Alianza, turn it against the Nationalist Party (with the reformist's typical, and pathetic timorousness, forced by history to "do something," but against the imperialists, despite itself) and focus the attention of the Nationalist Party on its leader and the country's on the Party.

The crisis that broke in the heart of the Empire on October 21, 1929, by the same imperialist mechanism that we pointed to, was felt in Puerto Rico years before. The signs of unhappiness in Puerto Rico were, for example, the struggle of the *Asociación de Agricultores* (Farmers Association) against the Alianza, the growth of the membership of the masses within the Partido Socialista, the high number of members that had joined the *Federación Libre de Trabajadores* (Free Federation of

---

33 The time is 1949.

Workers). Neither the *Asociación de Agricultores*, nor the *Partido Socialista*, nor the *Federación Libre de Trabajadores* were instruments for liberation. But the people, unhappy and disoriented, were seeking tools for struggle. In this sense, the factors already highlighted revealed the uneasiness within the country.

Such uneasiness could only be reflected inside the Alianza. And it began to show with that organization's hesitation, timidity, and cowardly acts. In the midst of 1927, the colonial legislature met to receive a hero of the moment; a United States Air Force Colonel: Charles Lindbergh. With him, they sent a message—which he delivered—to the government of the United States that quoted the deceptive proclamation written by General Miles to the Puerto Ricans upon the invasion in 1898. Politely, the legislature requested a solution to the status of Puerto Rico. President Coolidge responded: "The United States has made no promises to the people of Puerto Rico that it has not already fulfilled completely."

Weakening, Senate President, [Antonio] Barceló, and House President, José Tous Soto, sent a message to Coolidge, exhorting him to seek Congress' passing of legislation that would allow Puerto Rico to elect a governor. In January of 1928, as the Pan-American Conference was taking place in Havana, Barceló and Tous Soto requested that the United States turn Puerto Rico into a "Free State". All of those symptoms, weak as they were, were signs of the need for independence and of the incapacity of the Alianza leaders to guide the country along the path to satisfy its needs. They were the fearful preamble to the great independence movement that would succeed them.

But such timidity alerted the imperialists to the danger that the *Alianza* could pose for them. Confident that the independence movement had been eliminated, the rulers chose to overlook the agglutination of the great masses of Puerto Ricans into one political party, opening the way to colonial administration. For the United States, the *Alianza* became—through historical law—a party that must be destroyed, before the same law could turn it into a united force under new leadership that could overturn colonial rule in Puerto Rico; and so, it destroyed the *Alianza*.

But the empire had to postpone an immediate action, because it was busy and preoccupied dealing with the "threat" of Al Smith—a

Catholic—as presidential candidate. But once Smith lost and Herbert Hoover became president, it turned its attention again to Puerto Rico to get rid of the problem by nurturing divisiveness.

The first step was to make up another political force to support against the Alianza. And indeed, against the Alianza that had won the elections of 1928. A coalition of minority forces named *Grupo de Buen Gobierno* (Group for Good Government) composed by republicans from the *Partido Republicano Puro* and the *Partido Socialista*—all annexationists—was put together under the leadership of Rafael Martínez Nadal and Santiago Iglesias Pantín, respectively. They came together to uphold the colonial status.

Colonel Roosevelt transferred colonial management to the Group for Good Government. The Alianza fell apart. All of its efforts to take hold of the colonial "power" were useless because the needs of the imperialists were a priority. The fate of the Alianza proved that the attainment of real political power in the colony was not possible. And that to insert itself in the existing political game—which is the imperialist game—was not useful for the good of the country but only for the service of the Empire.

When the Alianza disintegrated, a great portion of the once Historical Republicans went over to the Pure Republicans' side, who were then enjoying the administration of the colonial budget. Barceló and the old Partido Unión leaders undertook the futile task of reviving that party. But that ended with a "rest in peace" decision from the imperialist courts. The Partido Liberal, which was born of the demise of the Partido Unión, became something else and was in consequence, the militant, fearless and liberating insurgency of the Partido Nacionalista de Puerto Rico.

We will delve into the years of greater struggle, dynamic interests and most creative work that we witnessed. Pressured from below by the nascent revolutionary forces, despised by the masters, the Alianza's reformism gave way—not as the Empire had thought—to blatant annexationism, but to a true rebirth of national consciousness. Puerto Rico then definitively joined the Latin American anti-imperialist camp, and began to act, jointly with Sandinism, in the front line of fire.

9

REBIRTH OF NATIONAL CONSCIOUSNESS

If a close look at Puerto Rico's history in the nineteenth century is equivalent to a careful examination of the history of the struggle for Puerto Rican independence, to examine the history of Puerto Rico's struggle for independence during the period we will deal with in this chapter is also equivalent to scrutinizing the history of the Nationalist Party. We will find a true national rebirth, with struggles, social unrest, discovery of patriotic thought and massacres, sublime sacrifices and terrible treachery; unparalleled heroism and murders committed cowardly. In synthesis, all of the manifestations of a rebirth of the national consciousness of a people subjected to colonialism by imperialism, and that, in spite of its great efforts, adverse circumstances that it was unable to overcome, prevented it from attaining victory.

Because this period is of the recent past, and because it will be treated in another work titled *The Glorious Years*, [34] its details will not be discussed here. We will limit ourselves to lay the foundation that supports our thesis.

Since its foundation in 1923, the Nationalist Party languished in an excessively juridical and academic life, distanced from the people it wished to liberate. But nevertheless, it had a profound importance since its inception. It was the first party founded in Puerto Rico with the sole purpose of defending national independence.

But that party underwent a sudden transformation in 1930. The causes for this change may be synthesized by the following quote from [Cuban] José Martí: "Sometimes the leader is ready and the people are not; at times the people are ready and the leader cannot be found." If we look closely at the events that took place that year, we shall see the people's

---

34 The book was never written.

readiness coinciding with the presence of the leader, to launch a new period in the struggle for independence.

It is the coincidence of both factors—readiness of both leader and people—which explains the sudden transformation of the Nationalist Party and the glorious journey lived by the people of Puerto Rico under its guidance during that unforgettable decade.

On September 13, 1928, the fury of hurricane San Felipe devastated the country. It entered through the eastern coast and took a destructive path throughout the entire [insular] territory as it moved towards the West to exit. The country was left in ruins.

Thirteen months later—October 1929—the Stock Market in New York collapsed. It was the beginning of the crisis inherent in the cycle of United States capitalism. The repercussions in the colony highlighted. Before the fall of the market, the United States had thrust upon the colony its imminent crisis, but then it fell with all the weight of an apocalyptic monster over a defenseless populace.

Quietly, something new began to quicken in the country's belly. The old leadership was absolutely incapable of rising to the occasion. The people themselves could not immediately find the way to satisfy their needs. No one dared to speak "Sovereignty!" And if said, it was spoken with a weak monotonous singsong of defeat and despair. The country needed a voice that would command it to listen to the demands for justice. A new, plain, brutally frank voice, with the clarity that the country had yet to understand; the brutal frankness that detracts from all the half gestures, from all the marginal insinuations, the cowardly palliatives, the trembling innuendos of the colonial half tongue. It needed a voice that would shout for redemption, for starting the national machinery onto new paths.

January 1930 was the precise moment, when a native of Ponce, Pedro Albizu Campos, returned to Puerto Rico, after three years of travel through Latin America, on a mission of the Nationalist Party.

The party had relegated its best man, Albizu, to an unimportant role for six years. Clearly, the man had been ready, but not his people. But, upon his return, the people were ready and the man could no longer be denied his importance as a leader. During the Party's convention of May 1930, the rank and file overcame the leadership, and Albizu Campos was selected to lead the movement. Leader and masses came together to begin a new stage of struggle for independence.

Since his return from that Latin American trip, which had really been an exile, his speeches greatly moved the most alert sectors of the population. The young, the honest intellectuals aligned themselves with him. Many voices and pens began to speak out and write inspired by Pedro Albizu Campos. Writers and artists, teachers and intellectual professionals, honored him in public. On the streets, on the roads, in the buses, and in public places, the people would surround him. The most notable career of any public man in Puerto Rico had begun.

Albizu Campos had dared to utter the word: "independence" in a unique way. He pronounced a magic word: "Revolution". Both really synthesized his doctrine and practice, and this is proof that the attitude of the Puerto Rican people, when faced with those two key words, and of why we have stated that in 1930 the people were ready and the leader was there to launch a new period of struggle for independence.

With extraordinary excellence, the Party not only increased the membership at a fast pace, and the quality of its members, taking in the thought and sensitivity of the leader, tempered by a heroic sense of history in the concept about sacrifice, in the personal disposition to place the interests of the country—to be served by life and property—above all individual or secondary interest. This meant the rebirth of the tradition of Lares.

It is fitting then to ask: Why didn't Puerto Rico, with Albizu Campos and the Nationalist Party as instruments, become independent? That period must be judged in accordance with the knowledge of historic laws, and of the ebb and flow always present in historical processes. With that perspective the magnitude, greatness, and durability of that liberating period of the Nationalist Party during the third decade of this century, comes through, and therein is the crystal clear explanation why, without being a dark mystery, nor gibberish, nor absurd frustration, that the struggle did not lead to victory. It is necessary to look at history as a process and not as a roster of names and events that begin and take place at random.

For the sake of clarity, we will divide that period of struggle in five different parts that were the consequence of the historical ebb and flow.

When the revolution was strong, reaction was in retreat; and when reaction was at a peak, revolution was weak:

16. November of 1932 to January of 1934, reaction was strong.
17. January until May 1934, revolution was strong.
18. May 1934 until September of 1935, reaction was strong.
19. September 1935 until 1937, revolution was strong.

We will examine how the forces of revolution and reaction shifted during those periods. The revolutionaries were the Nationalist Party and the constant or periodically available forces were influenced, moved or thrust into the struggle by the Party's struggle. The reactionary forces were Imperialism and all those who constantly or periodically served it.

From 1930 to 1932

Pedro Albizu Campos returned in January to find the already mentioned conditions and effects. By May, he was formally and, in fact, the chief of the revolutionary movement. The party had adopted a revolutionary program that included participation in elections. It registered with the commitment of proclaiming the Republic and calling for a Constitutional Assembly, following the victory at election time. Intense campaigning began. The old annexationist party, the Partido Republicano Puro, added independence to its platform.

The Partido Liberal was founded, claiming to be independentist, but essentially and in practice, collaborationist and reformist. The Nationalist Party was ahead in the country's political scene. In April of 1932, the government, aware that it was losing ground, resorted to an act of open provocation. The colonial legislature began to consider a bill that would make the Puerto Rican flag, the official flag of the colony. On April 16, the Nationalists reacted to the legislature's move.

Under Albizu Campos's leadership, an assault on the Capitol building by Party members and people in general evicted the legislators. Nationalism gained its first martyr: Ángel Manuel Suárez Díaz. There were many men and women wounded. The government retreated but accused Albizu Campos of mutiny. A Puerto Rican judge exonerated him. But the government gave up on the proposition to dishonor the flag. In November, the Party went to elections and was defeated.

What happened? To arrive at the right answer it is important to keep in mind the fundamental thesis of this work: That there are two tendencies, the revolutionary, at the service of the people's needs; and the reformist, which serves imperialism. Both had been struggling against each other in the Puerto Rican political thought.

The Nationalist Party, headed by Albizu for eighteen months, did not have the time to set deep enough roots into the popular masses' hearts and minds to definitely embed its clarifying doctrine. United States Imperialism, conversely, mobilized to its ranks two forces that should have supported the Nationalist Party: the workers in the ranks of the Partido Socialista and the harassed remnant of the criollo sugar cane plantation owners and their tenant farmers in the Partido Liberal. The leadership of both parties was determining their political paths–or better said–detouring it.

In a previous chapter concerning we described the character of the Partido Socialista, extensively. We will point out, however, to an observation made in 1931 by Professor Bailey W. Diffie on page 196 of his book, Porto Rico: A Broken Pledge (Vanguard Press, New York): "The similarity between the language of the Socialists and that of other parties, shows that the origins of the Nationalist and Socialist parties are closely related. Both come from the understanding that one of the basic evils of the imperialist economic system is found in the amazingly extensive absenteeism [of the land owners]."

In previous pages Diffie quoted in part the 1930 Nationalist program: "Under the hard yoke of North American colonialism, from a nation of owners we have become a mass of farm hands, a rich mine for exploitation by the invading capital."

"The Nationalist Party ... will organize the workers to obtain from the foreign or invading interests the [economic] participation that they are entitled to... It will try by all means to make non residents [of Puerto Rico] bear the larger portion of the economic burden, to destroy the system of large estates of land holdings and absenteeism, and to divide real estate among the greater number possible of landowners..."

It should be emphasized that the basic needs of the people were then as they are now. What were they? Independence and social justice, which are as inseparable now as independence and abolition of slavery were in the nineteenth century. All of the ideals of nationhood have remained dependent upon those two basic needs, which must be grabbed directly, without fail, without opportunistic hesitations.

The Partido Socialista preached social justice and trust in the United States. It painted an idyllic portrait of social justice attained without struggle, by just winning an election and requesting it from Washington who, generously would rush to grant it without delay. Based on the undeniable truth that independence was the instrument of social justice, the Partido Nacionalista told the truth about the nature of the struggle necessary to obtain it: a hard fight for life or death, against the arrogant United States Imperialism.

Progressively, in the heat of battle and in its propaganda, the Nationalist Party, obfuscated with the fight for independence, relegated social justice to one side. It was a slip, but a very unfortunate one. At the critical point in the struggle, using a criticism made by Albizu as an excuse, the daily El Mundo closed access of its pages (it was the only newspaper with countrywide circulation) to Nationalist propaganda. Without excuses, the radio stations, controlled by the federal government, refused to broadcast Nationalist propaganda. The working masses, deceived by the reformist leadership of the Washington backed Partido Socialista, were thus deprived in equal intensity of Nationalist propaganda and abandoned it although it guaranteed victory, and were drawn instead to the spurious socialism.

On the other hand, Imperialism found its best supporter in the "independentist" Partido Liberal, born of two contradictory stimuli: the Nationalist Party's campaign that had drawn the masses and given them élan and the financial backing of the United States Government and [Washington's] electoral guarantees. Led by the once chief of the Partido Unionista, a businessman from Fajardo, Antonio Barceló, (although only in name, because Muñoz Rivera was the real power), and really, the leader of the Alianza [Puertorriqueña].

Barceló and the leadership of the Partido Unionista had been trying to revive that party. A court judgment prohibited them from using the name and its insignias, due to a technicality, left them without a name. Then, they received the financial support from the United States investors as an instrument for dividing the forces in favor of independence. And, truly, the importance of the Partido Liberal's service to the Empire, while invoking "independence" cannot be emphasized enough.

The Partido Liberal presented the same problem as the Partido Socialista. The Partido Nacionalista, aware of the nature of the struggle, was getting the people ready for a fight to the ultimate consequences, the Partido Liberal gave public speeches and broadcast propaganda offering independence in exchange for votes. Both the Liberal and the Socialist parties portrayed Washington as generous and willing to grant independence to the asking. The majority of the independentist masses, deceived by that propaganda, voted for the Partido Liberal.

For the elections of 1932, the Partido Nacionalista was asking of the people to give a mandate for revolution. The Socialists and Liberals were asking for permission to deceive them.

The people were ready to fight for independence and its consequent social justice, but were prevented from receiving the clear message on time about the tactics for battle. It was then possible for the reformist leadership to confuse and divide in favor of Imperialism. Once more, reformism betrayed the country on behalf of the Empire.

The reformist leadership made up of Socialists and Liberals had the power bestowed on them by Imperialism: the police, the army, the bureaucracy, investors, and banking. Disgraceful puppets of the invading power, they ensured the life of Imperialism in Puerto Rico when it was, for the first time, seriously threatened.

The result of the November of 1932 elections shifted the country from an upturn in the revolutionary movement to a peak for the reactionary forces. The election of Franklin D. Roosevelt to the presidency of the United States, unexpectedly strengthened the reactionaries in Puerto Rico. This statement may seem incorrect, given the worldwide prestige as to the progressiveness held by the most capable of the United States' imperialist chiefs. But as we describe the years of struggle [in the 1930s], it will become evident that the progressive atmosphere in the metropolis became so reactionary in Puerto Rico that it was the first time, since the invasion of Puerto Rico by the United States, that assassination was employed openly to maintain colonial rule.

In the elections of 1932, the Partido Liberal won its massive support through the enthusiasm for independence created by the Nationalists' campaign, and the Partido Liberal's economic power because of fear within the sectors that sold out to Imperialism, also caused by the Nationalist campaign. The Partido Liberal stood out, individually, as the strongest party, but it lost the election, becoming a minority in the colonial legislature. The election was won by a coalition of the Partido Unión Republicana and the Partido Socialista. Unión Republicana was the pro-annexation party and the most reactionary in the country. On its own, it could not garner the masses to win an election except in a few towns, but riding on the wagon of the Partido Socialista, while holding the reins, it was able to participate in the electoral victory. The Socialist masses, spurred by the lengthy campaign of the Nationalists on behalf of social justice, energized by the campaign, assured electoral triumph and ideological failure.

November 1932 to January 1934

The Partido Liberal disintegrated after losing the election. But the Partido Nacionalista, although defeated at the polls, remained united and immediately began its new campaign with a stronger tone and a deeper thrust. The increase in the public that attended its meetings made it evident that the Party was about to enter a new period of growth. Hundreds of former affiliates of the Partido Liberal began to flock towards Nationalism. The unity of the liberating forces under the leadership of Pedro Albizu Campos was predictable.

The Empire was not going to allow this. Roosevelt's "progressiveness" rammed against Puerto Rico to strengthen the reactionaries, and infuse energy into reformism with a full force campaign of demagoguery and bribery worse than any people have been subjected to. It was then that the federal "rehabilitation" agencies were created: The Federal Emergency Relief Administration (FERA), the Puerto Rico Emergency Relief Administration (PRERA), and the Puerto Rico Relief Administration (PRRA).

The programmed bribery was clear. The "Coalition" (of Unión Republicana and Socialists), having won the elections, had full access to the colonial insular budget, gathered by the taxes imposed upon the inhabitants. The vanity of the Coalition's leaders would be satisfied with "honors" received through access to positions in the colonial government.

The "danger" lay in that the masses of the Partido Liberal—independentists who had been lead by a reformist leadership at the service of Imperialism—could rush to join the Nationalist party. In order to avert that the Empire created the federal agencies in order to give the Partido Liberal the millions for those budgets. It is noteworthy that the millions were given to the independentist sector of the Liberals, headed by Luis Muñoz Marín, and not to Barceló and his coterie of ultra conservatives.

Washington's plan was very clear. On the one hand it kept the coalitionists and liberals divided by nurturing the hatred and the budgetary war between them. And on the other, it created a division within the Partido Liberal. Above all, it gave the appearance of a Federal Government friendly towards the independentists in the Partido Liberal, gaining thus the trust of the people in their despotic practices and stopping the shift of the liberal forces to the Partido Nacionalista.

The result was an upturn of treachery and reformism, and the glorification of Imperialism by the coalitionist leadership, who was enjoying the insular budget; and by the liberal leadership, who was managing the budget of the federal agencies established in the Island. The Empire's plan was a long-term division of the country.

Between January and March of 1934

The United States could not solve its economic crisis as easily as it accomplished the political division of the Puerto Ricans. [In fact], their economic crisis was getting worse. The repercussions on the working masses and peasants of Puerto Rico could not be avoided with the transfer of the funds that kept alive—and at the service of Imperialism—the native sugar plantation owning bourgeoisie with which large sectors of the middle class were bribed.

In January of 1934 the sugar cane industry workers went on strike. The reformists who embraced the Gompers style of labor unions and who made up the Federación Libre de Trabajadores Puertorriqueños rushed, as they had always done in the past, to take over the strike's leadership. To the Imperialists' and the entire country's surprise, the workers rejected them. Instead, they called upon Pedro Albizu Campos to lead their strike. This automatically changed the nature of the strike from a strike for economic improvement to a political one.

The Empire shuddered. That unexpected occurrence gave unusual power to the Partido Nacionalista, Political power, for the first time at its reach, to instill the idea of independence in the workers and peasants. The United States knew that the acceptance of the idea of independence by those sectors meant the attainment of independence for Puerto Rico.

That first coordination between the national leadership for independence and the workers of the imperialist-colonial regime's main industry, produced the first great back down of Imperialism in Puerto Rico. This was a lesson that Independentists have forgotten and should not have. Imperialism has not, however, and has never been careless again.

The manner in which that strike was handled is revealing. The representative chosen by the absentee mill owners, was not a lawyer, nor an employer, nor a member of the *Asociación de Productores de Azúcar* (Association of Sugar Producers). It was Colonel E. Francis Riggs, of the United States Army and Puerto Rico's Chief of Police. During an interview he requested of Albizu—arranged by independentist engineer Félix Benítez Rexach—Riggs admitted to Albizu that the strike was just and recommended that the employers end the strike immediately by granting the demands of the workers. And the strike was resolved.

The sugar cane workers strike that took place from January to May of 1934 created a crisis for colonial rule and is an unequaled event in the history of Puerto Rico's struggle for independence. The strike brought together for the first time in a revolutionary alliance, the working and the middle classes in order to fight for a common goal. It should have resulted in the consolidation of a revolutionary alliance for independence.

What prevented it? In fairness to the participants, let us analyze the reasons that prevented that consolidation. The Partido Nacionalista did not have leaders who were knowledgeable of labor organizing. The social origins of the party's leadership were a heavy tragedy for its possibilities and the fate of the Nation. With an unselfish, heroic and noble gesture the nationalist leadership assured the economic victory for the striking workers, but it was not able to displace the leadership of the Federación Libre de Trabajadores and organize a new labor union with a patriotic spirit, although it tried. But that happened a year too late. The Empire recovered from the blow and declared war on the party.

The spontaneous movement, born of the working class, certainly took place among the laborers of the country's main industry. But therein lies the reason for its absolute disorganization, because having trusted the treacherous leadership of the *Federación Libre*, that leadership had left the field workers of the sugar cane industry totally disorganized. That is explicable, since that organization was not against Imperialism. Therefore, not even a ghost of a sugar labor union existed to become a starting point for a labor union. An organization had to be formed to teach the basic principles of trade union struggle. Therefore, it is not necessary to stress the political backwardness that plagued the sugar cane workers. The weakness of the working class, coupled with the already mentioned prevalent conditions within the Partido Nacionalista, could only lead to the missed opportunity in consolidating an alliance between the working and the middle classes to liberate Puerto Rico.

And all the details can be summarized in a single one: With the dismemberment of the Partido Socialista, the working class lacked a political party of its own, ideologically mature and capable of organizing it and guiding the consolidation of that healthy and mutually convenient revolutionary alliance with the middle class in order to free the country from colonialism. Had those conditions existed, the history of Puerto Rico would have been different. We would not only have been free, but perhaps, instead, the first popular democracy in the New World.

When the consequences of that circumstantial alliance were lost in organizational emptiness, the Empire was relieved. And prepared the most fierce offensive that the Puerto Rican people have had to endure. And endure it did with heroic courage, patriotic arrogance that we may be proud of. But it was not feasible to crown it with victory. Old and new obstacles came together to keep us away from winning.

Between May 1934 and September 1935

The period between May 1934—when the strike ended—and September of 1935, the reactionaries recovered from the blow of the strike and began their brutal offensive to eliminate the Partido Nacionalista, behead the independence movement in the country and assure, according to plan, a long period of reactionary dominance, of imperialist "law and order," and the destruction of Puerto Rican nationhood.

For the revolutionary forces this was a period of silence, of anguish, of agonizing struggle so that the imminent storm that we all felt looming upon us would not find us defenseless. An outstanding event marked the stance of each faction: the strength of the reactionaries, and the lack of guided preparation on the part of the revolutionaries for the great blow that was to come. During mid 1934, United States President, Franklin D. Roosevelt made a spectacular imperial visit to Puerto Rico. The regime used all the resources available to make it a grand visit, to obtain the desired effects of having Caesar set his imperial foot on the colony, and to reaffirm imperial power in order to impress and agglutinate all the forces allied to Imperialism, and to overwhelm the country and intimidate the revolutionaries and patriots. But underneath all the show of strength a deep fear of loss was present. The mobilizations of the armed forces, the intensity of police vigilance [of the citizenry] were undoubtedly a sign of governmental worry. It was evident that the precautions were taken not only because a chief of state was present. Everyone felt that something more was brewing. The Partido Nacionalista declared the Imperial Chief "persona non grata".

The nature of the struggle during that period makes it hard to tell the story of the process, and it is even harder for this writer. The Partido Nacionalista sent me abroad. I returned nine months later, and the way I was received revealed the character of the existing situation. The few comrades who knew of my return, went to greet me at the pier. But for each one of us, there were six government henchmen.

During my absence, the Government had made great efforts to destroy the Party "from within," through the infiltration of supposed "discontents" with the Party's policies. The situation was such that the Government concluded that the Party had been practically disbanded. Two months after my return, I had the joy, and the Government the disappointment, of confirming that the opposite was true. On September 23, 1935, anniversary of the Lares Revolution, in the historic birthplace of the First Republic of Puerto Rico, the Party demonstrated its strength and discipline.

September 1935 to June 1937

The demonstration at Lares was the result of great efforts at organization and mobilization. It was a show of the great need that the [Nationalist] Party itself had to prove that despite the desertions, its power and strength had not been harmed. That had an indisputable positive effect, because the membership regained its faith. The cohesion resulting from its efforts to garner energies and resources; the solidarity and daring displayed on that day at Lares, prepared the Party for the great fight that would soon follow.

On the other hand, although the propitiatory effect of the act at Lares cannot be denied, it is also true that it made the Government launch an armed attack. The Lares demonstration jolted the Government from its premature illusions. Clearly, it was not true that it had disbanded the Party. On the contrary, the strength of the demonstration and the significant incidents that took place at Lares that day, were proof that the Party had come out of the ordeal more united, better organized and strengthened in its will to struggle. So the government decided to launch its armed attack one month and one day after, on October 24, 1935.

In effect, on that date, the government murdered in the town of Río Piedras, the Labor Secretary of the Party, Ramón S. Pagán; the Cadets' Lieutenant, José Santiago Barea, and four other party members. Another, Dionisio Pearson was seriously wounded.

The act at Lares was the mark of a new revolutionary upturn. The most intense and profound in the history of Puerto Ricans as a people since the turn of the [twentieth] century. The most intense and profound in terms of catalytic strength and creative results.

The morning of October 25, 1935—the day after the killings—the Junta Nacional, the Party's executive board, called a meeting in Aguas Buenas. All the presidents and secretaries of the municipal boards attended. At the meeting, a new organizational plan was approved. I was elected Secretary General and Luis F. Velázquez was chosen National Treasurer.

The national mourning demonstrated on that afternoon was in itself a categorical response to the government, not only on the part of the Party but also on the part of the people. The use of political assassination by the government to destroy the Party became a challenge. As such it was addressed by Albizu in his speech at the Seboruco cemetery, and in the document issued by the organization, signed by Albizu and myself, that appeared in the newspaper La Palabra, which I directed. But the challenge was also picked up by the people who attended, in the thousands, to walk with the dead martyrs murdered in Río Piedras to their final resting place. From that moment on, the Party received larger monetary contributions and the people treated its leadership with greater sympathy and affection in general.

The brutal murders committed on October 24 by the government, and the party's response to it, galvanized the people. And life in Puerto Rico began to have an accelerated historic rhythm, a revival of national pulse. This journey, even when considered in its minimal aspects, is of great and unmatched importance as an experience for the people of Puerto Rico, proof that Puerto Ricans had enormous revolutionary potential that, as a consequence of what happened then, is today greater, wider, stronger and deeper than ever before, [35] and have what is needed to free Puerto Rico.

The Río Piedras Massacre gave the Party its first newspaper for the masses: La Palabra, founded on October 19, 1935—five days before the killings—its second edition sold ten thousand copies. It kept the party under the necessary tension and the people informed of the details and the intensity of the struggle, which increased from day to day with clashes in many towns.

The incident at Río Piedras and the courage with which the Party faced the aggression reopened the pages of the dailies El Mundo and El Imparcial. The latter embarked on an intense pro-independence editorial campaign and became a leader among Puerto Rican daily newspapers in supporting the right to independence, and leading in sales.

---

35 The year is 1949.

With the Massacre and the Party's valiant response, the propaganda in the international arena begun in 1930 produced the desired effect. Unprecedented campaigns in favor of the independence of Puerto Rico began in all of Latin America and the Spanish Republic. The case of Puerto Rico definitely acquired the international publicity it deserved. The news blockade imposed by the United States was broken.

Since the killings at Río Piedras the Party entered into its true mode of vanguard in the fight for independence, gaining direct access to the populace and providing it with leadership. It was the time when a true base for a national anti-imperialist front was established. The country was ready for the coming events.

On February 23, 1936, Colonel Riggs, Chief of Police and responsible for the Río Piedras Massacre who had publicly declared "war, war, and war against the Nationalists," was shot to death in San Juan through the heroic acts of Elías Beauchamp and his comrade and friend Hiram Rosado. They were arrested, taken to the police headquarters, and, by the command of Colonel Cole, chief of the 65th Infantry Regiment of the United States Army, executed in cold blood. Weeks later, President Roosevelt promoted Colonel Cole to Brigadier and transferred him to the United States.

A new wave of patriotic intensity filled the national soul. The people's presence at the funeral of both heroes and martyrs exceeded that of any public function ever held before in Puerto Rico. The people under the leadership of the Partido Nacionalista glorified the two heroes. Hundreds of thousands of pictures of Elías Beauchamp and Hiram Rosado appeared in people's homes.

The government was stunned. With the exception of the immediate reaction caused by Colonel Cole's order—given from the fortress of El Morro, which he did not leave except to attend Colonel Riggs' funeral and to travel to the United States—and the police's assault on *La Palabra*, half hour after the murders, the government's action, including that of General [Blanton] Winship and all of United States officialdom [in the Island and the Mainland], was frankly cowardly.

Fear of the people made the government think things over. After six weeks of hesitation, it changed tactics. On March 31, the Federal Court issued a *sub poena duces tecum* [36] that had immediate effects. On April 2, 1936, the Secretary General [37] of the Party was jailed for refusing to comply with the imperial court's order. He was sent to jail for one year for contempt of court. But his imprisonment did not diminish the numbers in the party, nor the people's adhesion to it. On the contrary, the ranks felt more self-assured by the leadership's loyalty. Party members and people in general gathered in great numbers in front of the jail, not only on visiting days, but every day. Political unrest increased in intensity, rallying new and wider sectors around the national banner.

This became even more intense when, a few days later, judicial proceedings began against the President of the Party, Pedro Albizu Campos, the Secretary General, Juan Antonio Corretjer (already incarcerated), the National Treasurer, Luis F. Velázquez; and other leaders: Clemente Soto Vélez, Pablo Rosado Ortiz, Juan Gallardo Santiago, and Julio Héctor Velázquez, for "conspiracy to overthrow the government of the United States by of force". A bail in the amount of one million dollars was imposed on the accused, and it was paid in a few hours. All of the accused were freed provisionally, except Corretjer, who was extinguishing a contempt sentence.

Faced with an unexpected public opinion, the government used another trick. Senator Millard Tydings proposed a bill to recognize independence for Puerto Rico. The day after the outburst of the news, the information agencies in the United States broadcast throughout the country a statement from the office of President Roosevelt, informing the country that the Tydings Bill had been filed with the previous consultation and agreement of President Roosevelt, his cabinet and the congressional leaders.

There was a burst of joy all over the country. The United States flag disappeared from more that three quarters of the municipal centers of government. Students and people in general demonstrated in the streets. The leader for annexation, Rafael Martínez Nadal, made a public speech calling for his followers to embrace the struggle for independence since the United States had snubbed their annexation efforts.

---

36 Order to appear in a court of law and surrender documents pertaining to the Party.

37 The Author, Juan Antonio Corretjer.

The true meaning of the Tydings Bill was not understood by all. The Party, however, understood, but the Empire took for granted that neither the country, nor the Party would see through the maneuver.

Without a previous agreement, the Secretary General (from prison) wrote an article titled "La república de trapo" (The Puppet Republic) in which the Empire's deceit was dissected. From his headquarters Albizu issued the call for a Constituent.

What were the Empire's intentions in putting forth the Tydings Bill? On its own, Puerto Rico was moving towards independence. The prestige of the colonial imperialist institutions was tarnished. Evidently, the country was on its way to revolution and independence, through a process of its own, brought about by Puerto Rican forces, without taking into account the will and the institutional system of the Imperialists. Confronted with this situation, and persuaded that the struggle to submit the national movement by force of violence while the people favored it, the Empire changed its tactic, employing instead juridical repression. That change began with the sub poena duces tecum. With it, the Empire gave the appearance before the people of rectifying the murders and using its laws to reach an understanding with Nationalism.

The Tydings Bill and Roosevelt's showy statement, were meant—with equal malice—to convince the Puerto Rican people that they could resolve their constitutional problem by leaving the solution to the Empire. That is, it was meant to detour the national will, already on the road to solve its situation as the only depository of our sovereignty, to put back trust into the hands of Congress as depository of Puerto Rican sovereignty. And knowing that the Nationalist leadership would understand the maneuver for what it really was, but that the deceived populace would burst into independentist euphoria, provoking an unprepared armed insurrection, thus separating them from the great masses, which thought the status issue was resolved without further need for sacrifice. This would enable the Imperialists to repress fiercely and leave the country defenseless for a long time.

They counted on the Nationalist leadership to fall in their trap. Therefore, it postponed for more than two months the proceedings in the case against them for insurrectional conspiracy. But the Nationalist leadership, instead of falling, responded with revolutionary capability by calling for the Constituent, and inviting the leaders of all the political parties and the towns' mayors to subscribe to "A Call for the Constituent Assembly". The provocation was averted and the revolutionary process was on its way.

The pre-constituent process continued when the Empire, defeated, called for a trial. On July 30, the Nationalist leadership was sentenced to prison and exile for ten years. An appeal delayed their removal from the prison called La Princesa for ten months—until June 7, 1937—when they were transported to Atlanta, Georgia. All efforts to obtain bail for the Nationalists were in vain, as it was denied by all the courts of the United States, from the Federal Court in San Juan to Washington's Supreme Court.

The imprisonment of Albizu Campos on July 30, 1936, was a fatal blow for independence. That assured the division of the liberating forces, in favor of the imperialists and in detriment to the country, the loss of the opportunity for attaining independence at that period of the struggle.

An in effect, moved by the Nationalists' struggle, the greater part of the independentist masses, still under the spell of the Partido Liberal, followed the Nationalist slogans, and joined informally to the Party's struggle. The "radical wing" of the Partido Liberal took it practically over and, encouraged by the Nationalists' struggle, was increasingly daring. But once Albizu was incarcerated, the liberal leadership were unnerved. And so the shameful spectacle at the party's assembly in Yauco resulted in a minority headed by Antonio R. Barceló imposing its will over the majority lead by Muñoz Marín, and the party decided not to abstain from electoral participation, and it took the collaborationist road to elections.

The depth of abjection of Muñoz Marín's acquiescence in Yauco can be measured by the fact that despite his having raised his banner, the liberating impulse within the party's rank and file was so great that the non-participation in elections lost by a half vote. That fraction of a vote divided the independentists again, into revolutionary patriots and election advocating reformists; and with that half vote the necessary and sufficient unity to free Puerto Rico was lost. But the Partido Liberal and its leadership were soon punished, when they lost the elections they rushed to partake of—in order to legalize again the Empire's occupation of Puerto Rico—in November 1936. Later, the Partido Liberal was divided ignominiously by a boorish internal fight for a budget that made it disappear from the political arena. But to Puerto Rico's disgrace, some of those leaders survived and continued to sink the country further into colonial degradation.

On March 21, 1937, Imperialism celebrated the new division of the Puerto Ricans in Ponce. With premeditation, [then governor] Brigadier General Blanton Winship—with Washington's approval—executed the criminal Ponce Massacre. The horrific mass murder perpetrated on that day against the Nationalists and the people of Ponce in general, put the country on its feet again. The shock wave traveled the world. It even shook some people in the United States. And the government, which had prevented Congressman Vito Marcantonio from going to Puerto Rico in time to participate in the defense of the Nationalist leadership, hurried to allow the American Civil Liberties Union (ACLU) investigation. The search, intelligently done and carried out with honesty by Arthur Garfield Hayes, put the entire blame on the government of Brigadier General Winship. Nevertheless, that same government proceeded to try the Massacre survivors for murder. The prosecutor of Ponce's District Court, Rafael Pérez Marchand (then on the annexation camp, today an independentist) resigned to his post so as not to dishonor himself by participating in such infamy.

We recognize the American Civil Liberties Union, and Mr. Hayes has our eternal gratitude, but the historical truth is that the investigation carried out by that organization and Mr. Hayes' honesty were harmful to us. First, because it calmed the people, gave the Empire the opportunity to wait for the tension to subside, and, second, and the worst, because it strengthened reformism and reestablished trust in the Imperialists among the non-Nationalist sector of those who favored independence. We highlight that the Imperialists foresaw the beneficial result for them. We do, because Congressman Vito Marcantonio was not allowed to arrive on time to take part in the defense of the nationalist leadership, because it was not convenient for the Empire. It was feared that the presence of a United States congressman among the counsel for the defense would weigh heavily on the jury's decision, and because

Harold Ickes, then Secretary of the Interior, was a member of the Board of Directors of the American Civil Liberties Union.

As popular fury subsided with the aid of the American Civil Liberties Union investigation, the Supreme Court in Washington confirmed the sentence of the Nationalist leadership; and on June 7, 1937, they were transported to the Federal Penitentiary in Atlanta, Georgia. Two days later, Federal Judge Cooper, who had imposed sentence, was shot but not harmed. That attempt gave the government the excuse to incarcerate the first acting leadership of the Partido Nacionalista, presided by attorney Julio Pinto Gandía. After submitting a motion of *nolo contendere*, [38] Pinto Gandía and the other members of the interim leadership were sentenced to five years in prison, each to be extinguished in a different federal jail within the United States.

The revolutionary movement was halted, but not defeated. On July 25, 1938, national hero Ángel Esteban Antongiorgi gave up his life in Ponce when he opened fire against the unscrupulous and bloodthirsty general Blanton Winship to prevent him from delivering his speech of imperialist reaffirmation.

Those were the sounds of the last shots of a period in which the Puerto Rican will put to good use a truly superior strength. If was not enough to free Puerto Rico, there is no reason to think it was because of Imperialism's strength. Recognizing it as the strength of the only real enemy, we faced it in the same manner that we do now and will defeat it tomorrow. Do not look, either, with a mean spirit for defects and failures in the nationalist leadership, for it is easier to do that than look for the truth. And the truth has been deliberately hidden.

The revelation is inconvenient to some, to those who are benefitting from the dead at the Ponce Massacre, who today serve as miserable lackeys to the imperialists, with Luis Muñoz Marín at the lead. And those who continue to play at being independentists at the voting polls. But the real reason is that the electoral reformism of the "independentists" then, the liberals for independence "with law and order," "in peace and harmony," "enemies of violence," divided the basic forces on which the country was counting to become independent.

---

38 No contest

I am not defending my participation in that period of glorious struggle. The glory of leadership—and glory is accompanied by responsibility—has been given in its entirety by insiders and outsiders, to the president of the Partido Nacionalista, Albizu Campos. Today, I am not the party's secretary general as I was then. I am not even a member. I am defending the truth of that historic moment against a group of slandering cowards, simulators of patriotic fervor, and against the faultfinders who foresee all things... after they have happened, and about whom the greatest revolutionary of all time, Vladimir Ilich Lenin, wrote scathing prose, as they were the objects of his derision.

Neither am I affirming or denying that neither Albizu Campos nor I, nor the others who participated then in the leadership of the movement, did not make mistakes. Were there none? Wonderful! On with the fight! Were there any? It is lamentable, but when the shots are heard, it is time to close ranks and reproach the enemy, and do it with bullets.

I am not telling these truths, both glorious and bitter, because I seek glory as chronicler of my country's history. I killed and buried many years ago any ambition I might have had of gaining literary glory. I am telling these truths as a lesson that will help us all to face advantageously a great pain and a great danger: the enemy is wiping out our homeland and again the forces are divided between the electioneers [who preach] "law and order", "peace and harmony", "enemies of violence", enemies of electoral boycott, of resistance to the military conscription, of the gullible who trust that there can be an agreement with dignity with the United States following an electoral victory. Then there are those of us who are on the camp of Revolution. And Puerto Rico is approaching a great hour! May our beloved people open their eyes, discard a past of elections that is an unbroken roster of defeats, a precipice of frustrations; and stand up and follow the route to the revolutionary juncture that will guarantee independence! The guarantee of revolutionary victory means a united independence movement, a united people! And there is no use in dreaming about a one party based unity. That is equivalent to refusing to learn the truth. Words alone do not make unity. They do not bring together a people to wage great battles: the great battle that will be needed for our independence. People come together inspired by the great ideals of our nationhood and are moved to actions, each person deeply affected with love of life and disdain for death. Love of life in the immortality of the Nation and fearlessness of death as they face the danger that threatens the Homeland!

10

"BREAD, LAND, LIBERTY"

The struggle that Puerto Rico had just sustained against the United States had deep and specific effects. It destroyed part of the Empire's anti-nationhood efforts and awakened dormant creative energies within the people regarding national consciousness.

The conditions in which the struggle took place, and the way in which it developed impeded its logical growth under the direction of the nationalists and prevented advantageous results of the struggle to benefit the country: Albizu Campos was incarcerated and the [rest] of the political leadership was displaced onto the colonialist freedom killer, Luis Muñoz Marín.

The nationalist struggle discredited the colonialist leadership in the eyes of the masses. The logic of each of their positions, their lack of patriotism, and their lack of courage made them all—without exception—in a lesser or greater degree, allies of the government policies. Either by commission or by looking the other way when the killings were perpetrated by the Roosevelt administration through the acts of its representative General Blanton Winship. The people, having awakened from a deep colonial sleep, were disposed to reject them.

In the foul smelling pile of the colonialist confusion there was a man whose bad odor was less than the other [colonial servants]. That man was Luis Muñoz Marín. From very early on, he had demonstrated a strong ambition to lead. Also, since a very young age, he stood out for his self-confidence and interest in the labor movement. He saw in it a much further future than any of his contemporaries did, including Albizu Campos. He saw where the power and the future were. Regrettably for Puerto Rico, that man [Albizu Campos] did not see where the power lay so he could use it for the good of the country, nor did he see where the future lay to make it more fitting and beautiful for the good of his people. Who should have filled the gap that Albizu's imprisonment in Atlanta left—leading the country to independence in the juncture of the war—did not have the patriotism to undertake that great task. His lack of patriotism and his pathetic cowardice, took him along the path of detouring—as it had happened previously—the national energies towards serving Imperialism. For this reason, the colonial elections of 1940 did not mean the triumph of the *Partido Popular Democrático* (PPD) nor of Luis Muñoz Marín, and much less the victory of the Puerto Rican people, but the victory of United States Imperialism over the deceived and betrayed people of Puerto Rico. Those who speak of the degeneration of Luis Muñoz Marín and his lieutenants are mistaken. Now, as they are perched on the colonial budget, they are the same as they were before [accessing to power]. The only change has been one of degree. They were always reformists. The sickness of colonialism became worse in them until it turned them into traitors, openly and shamelessly.

Let's look at the composition of the forces that led Luis Muñoz Marín and his *Partido Popular Democrático* to the enjoyment of the opulent colonial budget.

1. The heroic struggle of the Nationalists revived the sentiments in favor of independence among the masses and discredited the colonialist political leadership, but was not able to prevent the imprisonment and exile of the [party's] leadership. It gave Muñoz Marín a wide, deeply moved and pure mass of people, and convinced the Empire that it was in its interest to support him in order to detour them politically.

2. The participation of Albizu Campos in the sugar industry strike of January 1934 showed that Santiago Iglesias Pantín's leadership of labor was worn out. And the Nationalists' struggle unleashed new energies within the working class, that inevitably were on the way to building a new tool for labor struggle, a new centralized labor union. This gave Muñoz Marín the opportunity to put forth a new labor concentration, stronger and more powerful than the previous one: the *Confederación General de Trabajadores de Puerto Rico* (CGT) or Puerto Rico Federation of Workers, which assured him an electoral base of workers and peasants.

Now, we will look at why the people of Puerto Rico decided to follow the leadership of Muñoz Marín, and why the United States government decided to support him.

In 1940, there were 55,519 farms. A little over half of them, 52.9 percent, consisted of less than 10 *cuerdas* (about 9.7 acres) each, occupying 7.6% of the total of all farms, 10.6% of cultivated lands, and they added to 6.9% of the total value of the lands, buildings, agricultural implements and machinery of all the farms in the country. There were 342 farms representing 0.6% of all the farms that had 500 *cuerdas* or more, and that made up a total of 30.9% of the total area occupied by farms and to 25.8% of the total area under cultivation. They represented 44.1% of the value of the lands, buildings, agricultural equipment and machinery of all the country's farms. This concentration of land holdings was prevalent in the best soils: the alluvial valleys and coastal and interior plains, dedicated mostly to sugar cane production. [39] That division of property of the lands was the result of the deformation of our economy by United States Imperialism. In consequence, that year, 69.6 percent of the population inhabited the rural areas. That is, 1,302,898 people, or more or less 230,000 families. Therefore, the great majority of rural families—around 80 percent of them—did not own land. They were families of farmhands who worked for wages and lived in housing that did not belong to them. [40] The depth of that tragedy is more acute when one is reminded of the fact that these conditions are under foreign domination, and monopolistic absentee landed estates. Remember, in 1900 Senator Foraker declared to the Senate in Washington: "The sugar and tobacco trusts already own practically all of the sugar and tobacco in Puerto Rico. [41] At the height of the war, when 70,000 young Puerto Rican men had been herded into the United States armed forces, and the United States Government was constructing many public works towards the war effort, "the coefficient derived from a 1941-42 study of 4,999 working class families yielded that there were 218 people employed for every 1,000

---

39 Félix Mejías, *Condiciones de vida de las clases jornaleras*, Junta Editorial de la Universidad de Puerto Rico, 1946.

40 Ibid.

41 Congressional Record, Volume 33, Part 3, Page 2,649, quoted by Mejías in his work: *Condiciones de vida de las clases jornaleras*, previously cited in Footnote 39.

inhabitants, including those in the age group of 10 to 14 years, who work for profit." [42] A larger sum of 287 per 1,000 was classified by Mejías as "probably the lowest coefficient in the civilized world."

By that time, the coefficients for the important nations of the world were: Soviet Union 580; France 520; Germany 490; United States 398; Cuba 320; Mexico 323 and Brazil 312. [43], [44]

In his study of the 1940 census, Mejías notes that there is a gap "in the population between the ages of 25 and 34, the most productive period for unskilled workers. In 1899, the population of Puerto Rico did not exhibit those characteristics. Probably, this was due to the incidence of tuberculosis." [45] Should we be surprised?

Those were the material conditions that served as a base for the upsurge of the Nationalist Party, and were later manipulated by the opportunistic reformist popular democrats by Muñoz Marín to detour the masses from the road to independence, which was, and still is, the key to solving the serious problems that afflict Puerto Rico. And those conditions were the product of the deformation created by Imperialism in the country's economy, made possible by the political domination that the United States Government has over the Puerto Rican people.

But the colonial reformist Luis Muñoz Marín and his *Partido Popular Democrático* chose, of course, an alliance with Imperialism, and diligently went to work in maintaining its hold on Puerto Rico. To do that, they used the oldest colonial reformist trick. They boldly and shamelessly adulterated the ideals of the Puerto Rican people with a most effective pretense. With demagoguery they raised the slogan of "Bread, Land and Liberty."

A people whose leadership was discredited to the point of contempt, who saw the leadership in whose hands it wanted to entrust its destiny disappear in the sky, transported by the Marines to a distant prison within

---

42 Op. cit. See Footnote 39.

43 Congressional Record, Volume 33, Part 3, Page 2,649, quoted by Mejías in his work: *Condiciones de vida de las clases jornaleras.*

44 Vicente Lombardo Toledano, *El proletariado de la América Latina ante los problemas del continente y del mundo,* Universidad Obrera de México, p. 37.

45 Year Book of Labor Statistics, Volume VII, International Labour Office, Montreal, Canada, 1943, page 5, quoted by Mejías in his work: *Condiciones de vida de las clases jornaleras.*

the invader country, and could not find, even within its own, immediate substitutes, whose thirst for independence was triggered by the heroic acts it had just lived through, who knew it was unarmed and disorganized; whose material needs shared the dinner table with hunger and with tuberculosis its marriage bed; who had not been able to make the collective tension last long enough so that the necessary cohesion would take place in order to make the great resolutions that precede great solutions; a people subjected to such conditions—and although painful to admit—is not surprising that it would let itself be seduced and betrayed once more, by a group of reformist opportunists that pretended to follow in the footsteps of the men who had been transported to Atlanta. They spoke of sacrifices, purity, abnegation and prudence, and flashed before the people the most revolutionary slogan invented by humankind, the slogan of the Russian Bolsheviks who had seized power in the great October Revolution; the slogan that sums up the struggle of all who are oppressed from the moment that primitive societies disintegrated: "Bread, Land and Liberty."

And this is better explained by remembering that the promise of the realization of that program that would free Puerto Rico from United States intervention, and also revolutionize Puerto Rican society, could be carried out without shedding a single tear, a single drop of blood if the people placed a paper vote in a poll on the day of elections in 1940. Of course, the human condition of trying to gain much with little effort, operating on a weakened people in its will to fight—would undoubtedly have the effects it did.

But, if the masses of people followed Muñoz Marín and his *Partido Popular Democrático* it was because the government of the United States allowed it. They would have not followed the PPD if the government would not have permitted it. This is by no means an indictment of the Puerto Rican People. It is an indictment against Luis Muñoz Marín and his accomplices, because if the government of the United States had launched against them the slightest hostility, neither Luis Muñoz Marín nor any of his accomplices would have dared confront that government. And they would have been crushed electorally by the reactionary forces mobilized against them by the Empire. Let us look at why the United States decided to support Muñoz Marín and his party.

1. Adolph Hitler, leading the fascist nations, was setting up a
    war against the oligarchies of the imperialist nations (United
    States, England, France, Belgium and Holland) in order to
    carve up the world for the fascists. By the middle of 1939,
    the economic war was ending. Concrete evidence of this was
    that in remote towns in Puerto Rico, cement produced in
    Hamburg could be found cheaper than Portland cement
    from the United States. The nearing of war posed to the
    United States, in all its dimensions, the issue, of imperial
    unity. This imperial unity for war was defined by Roosevelt
    with the vague phrase of "hemispheric solidarity." But the
    key to the Empire was rebelling. Nationalist agitation ran
    through the imperial tree of life.

    Organizations and popular congresses throughout Latin
    America, the parliaments of Argentina and Chile; the
    Constituent Assembly of Cuba; the Senate of the Dominican
    Republic, had all expressed solidarity with the Puerto Rican
    struggle for independence and were requesting of the govern-
    ment of the United States, and in particular of Roosevelt, the
    immediate release of the Nationalist leadership incarcerated in
    Atlanta. The Nationalist agitation did not stop. Within the
    country, even in July of 1938, the national question was being
    debated with bullets. And in 1939 refusal to comply with the
    imperialist compulsory military draft law was taking place.
    These were realities that the Empire could not take care of
    with a massacre or with a pedantic outburst. Latin America
    had to be appeased by pacifying the Puerto Ricans. Luis
    Muñoz Marín and his PPD were, to imperialism, the best
    candidates to carry it out. Undoubtedly, the United States was
    on target.

2. The appeasement of Latin America through the pacification
    of Puerto Rico required that the discredited colonial institu-
    tions gain prestige at all cost. It is a fact that the road towards
    independence is marked by the progressive discredit of the
    colonial institutions. Muñoz and his cadre represented,
    within the imperialist-colonial relations' framework, for

having been part of the "independentist wing" of the Partido Liberal, the only collaborationist group that had not become worn out in the previous phase of struggle. It was them who, given the opportunity, could better cooperate in the unworthy task of giving back prestige—in the eyes of the deceived populace—to the colonial institutions, beginning with that enslaving central institution, key to colonial subjugation: elections. So that, the more radical the PPD platform appeared to be, the better the Empire looked, and it was better for keeping the colony alive, because the greater trust in colonial institutions and in the United States handed back the people's trust to the Empire, who thus expected to clean up the mess it was in. This was evident in Muñoz Marín's propaganda. Note his constant endeavor to give the appearance of benevolence to the colonial institution, even to the point of denying that Puerto Rico is a colony.

3. The apparent radicalism of the PPD platform should have been constructed upon three basic points that corresponded to the three basic needs of the Puerto Ricans:

    a. The destruction of the absentee ownership of landed estates;

    b. Industrialization;

    c. Independence.

The falsehood of that platform, built however on the pressing needs of the nation, stood out due to the malicious and typically reformist investment placed on his points for struggle. For that program to be really radical, revolutionary and patriotic, it should have been offered on the basis of (1) fight for independence, and (2) based on a Constituent program that would eliminate the absentee estate holdings and industrialize the country, outside the electoral framework.

In another chapter we will examine in detail the subjugating, enslaving, imperialist, and anti-Puerto Rican character of the electoral system and the voting process in the present circumstances. Now, we will exclusively take a close look at the pretended anti-land-holding absenteeism and industrializing stance assumed then and supported by the PPD and [Luis] Muñoz Marín.

A.   The Land

Politics—declares the famous statement—is economy in a nutshell. The political power that governs Puerto Rico is not Puerto Rican. It responds to the United States. The so-called "Government of Puerto Rico" is a creation of the United States Congress. It is part of an administrative and repressive machinery belonging to the United States. Therefore, what governs Puerto Rico is not the Puerto Rican economy, but the economy of the United States.

The basic industry of the economy in Puerto Rico is sugar production. Wielding its political power, the United States invaded Puerto Rico in 1898 and since then has occupied it militarily. Through that political power it assimilated the Island's sugar industry. The native sugar industry became the property of the United States with only a small portion of it remaining in Puerto Rican hands.

The root of the land problem was the absentee estate holdings: the sugar cane lands held by people who lived in the United States. Definitely, the response mandated by the needs of Puerto Rico was the nationalization of the absentee estates. But nationalization presupposes having national political power. Therefore, the correct procedure is the fight for independence, which is equivalent to the struggle for the attainment of national political power that will enable the people to nationalize the sugar cane absentee estates.

Muñoz's PPD platform proposed the opposite. In essence he placed the cart before the horse. The results had to be the maintenance of colonialism, the prohibition to the people of Puerto Rico of exercising, with the conquest of independence, a necessary policy of nationalization.

The implementation of Muñoz and his party's colonial agrarian program has resulted in a net gain for the United States Government, which is an instrument of that country's financial oligarchy. The purchase of some of the land dedicated to the growing of sugar cane with public funds has double benefits for the Empire and is against the interests of the people of Puerto Rico.

1. The transfer of Puerto Rican land, purchased with Puerto Rican taxpayers' monies from the corporate interests of the United States, to the "government of Puerto Rico," which is the government of the United States, transferred the land from United States hands to United States hands and the loser was the Puerto Rican taxpayer. The seller United States corporation gets a high price for land it bought for a song and exploited without pity for some forty years—avoiding tax payments of as we all know—and once the purchase takes place and the transfer is made to the "Government of Puerto Rico" which is the same as the Government of the United States. The property stays in the same hands, adding with the transaction the monetary profit and greater political stronghold for government of the United States

2. The deception of the colonial-agrarian program of the PPD and Luis Muñoz Marín served, and continues to serve, the government of the United States in creating political confusion within the Puerto Rican people and detouring from independence.

3. The deceit of the colonial-agrarian program of the PPD and Muñoz Marín served to put blinders over the eyes of the Puerto Rican people so that they could not see that while there was talk of giving land to the peasants, the government expropriated the best lands in the country in favor of the United States Armed Forces. For example, [the islands of] Vieques and Culebra, [and lands in the towns of] Ceiba, Fajardo, Gurabo, [and those where] Camp Buchanan, Sabana Seca, Tortuguero, Punta Borinquen, and Losey Field are located. [All on] thousands of *cuerdas* of the best farming land that have gone into the hands of the United States military since the PPD won the elections in 1940.

The land problem posed to the people of Puerto Rico a decisive dilemma of independence or death. To propitiate domination, the United States, then and now, took the land that can feed the Puerto Ricans, literally, from under their feet. People without land go hungry. Landless people starve. Whether the land produces for subsistence or for industrial agriculture, it is the main source of food for all humankind. Absentee landlords that produce only one kind of crop are not concerned with the population of Puerto Rico, except, perhaps for the exclusive numbers who will lend their labor for exploitation in the cultivation of the lands. And even those—the Yankees think—can be substituted by others whenever convenient.

The rescue of our lands from the Yankee absentees and from the United States armed forces is equivalent to the seizure of our sovereignty from the government of the United States. The only way in which Puerto Rico could rescue its lands is through independence, because only the possession of sovereignty can give the people the political power to nationalize the absentee estates and direct its economy with motives, ends, purposes and conveniences that are exclusively Puerto Rican.

B.   Industrialization

The widening of Puerto Rican economic frontiers is attainable through industrial development. Colonialism is a straightjacket that curtails our potential for industrial development and inhibits industrialization. The colony stands out for its total industrial penury. It is nothing but a provider of raw materials. It is always a forced monopolized market for the metropolis' industries. The colony buys and imports more from the metropolis than it sells or exports to it.

Utilizing Muñoz Marín and his party, the United States tried to detour and undo the growing consciousness of the people of the need for industrialization by promising to do it under the United States flag. We shall proceed to prove how false, malicious and criminal that proposal was.

Democratic liberalism took hold in the thirteen English North American colonies in the eighteenth century because that was propitiated by their own development. And from this historical hybrid came forth the political document that conceived the United States: The Declaration of Independence.

But later, the Constitution of the United States was thought out, prepared, written and approved with a different purpose: to guarantee the economic growth of the merchant-farmers that the founding fathers of that country had become. The United States was conceived in freedom, but was born in slavery. Its revolution was betrayed.

The logical application of the Constitution followed inexorably the course of its practical realizations until it became the crisis that turned into the war of 1861. The triumph of the North in The Civil War did away with the fiction of sovereignty of the so-called "states" and confirmed definitively its provincial nature. It centralized the political power necessary to the development of industrial capitalism, brought the agricultural south to its knees and turned the industrialists into the indisputable owners of the government.

The great industrial growth took giant steps along the road opened by the Civil War. Not too many years passed in which the joining of industrial and banking capital was a fact, consolidating the dictatorial power of the financial oligarchy. Soon, the availability of capital launched the United States into a bold struggle between empires. The war with Spain made us the first victims.

In Paris, in 1899, and in open violation of every right, we were handed over to the barbaric jaws of the Yankee Imperialists. The possibility of industrialization for Puerto Rico was cut to the quick. In the colony, under the rule of the United States, all our potential lies in a catatonic state. This catatonia's only cure is independence.

It was in the face of that undeniable reality that Muñoz Marín presented, nine years ago, [46] his program for industrialization. And, although he has been the *criollo* leader at the service of imperialism for eight years, there has not been nor will there be industrial development in Puerto Rico as long as our country remains under the yoke of United States.

This is, of course, the reality of the inherent condition and monopolistic nature of the colonial-imperial regime that overwhelms the country. If the Constitution of the United States is the exclusive juridical basis for the hoarding acts of the Yankee financial oligarchy, needless to say Puerto Rico is automatically excluded from all opportunities for industrialization as long as it has not extricated itself from the political domination of the United States, as long as it has not conquered its independence. The entire

---

46 Operation Bootstrap was the industrialization program established by Muñoz Marín that forced massive flight of Puerto Ricans who were left without a livelihood.

repressive machinery falls like a catapult on any industrializing initiative on behalf of Puerto Rico. It may be appropriately said that the industrialization of Puerto Rico is unconstitutional from the standpoint of the United States. The state of Muñoz Marín's industrialization program could already be seen, as the colonialist messianism dissolved in the bitter sea of those realities. The process was divided in two parts.

1.   During the last war [World War II], it was in the best interest of the United States that in Puerto Rico a few small industries prosper, because the short-lived fostering of this small growth meant assistance to the war effort for the monopolies of the United States. That freed them from meeting some of the needs of Puerto Rico's captive market in order to attend to the needs of competing markets so that they could concentrate their efforts in winning the war. And victory would assure domination of the planet. The process planted greater conformism among Puerto Ricans with the colonial situation, and lent new prestige to the quite deteriorated colonial institutions. This diminished discontent and political unrest in the colony, and helped imperialism to drain away the Puerto Ricans' aspirations of freedom.

But the Empire's program would not prosper without struggle. Puerto Rico's panorama during those days had a strange side. Antagonistic forces strive for dominance within the bosom of human society that creates changes necessary for progress. The progress of economy and society demand change in the existing regime for another one, more in tune with the degree of development achieved by the productive forces. But the dominant classes who exploit, the ones who derive their privileges from the misery and ruin of the majority, do all they can to impede and retard the change, while those who suffer fight to achieve change as soon as possible.

It is necessary to point out, however, that within the exploiting privileged classes, there are nuclei of more or less reactionary sectors, and within the exploited classes there are cells of revolutionaries, reformists and counter revolutionaries. The latter, unfortunately, collaborate with the reactionaries and delay changes.

Thus, during the war years we see how in Puerto Rico a sector of the ultra reactionaries comes together to fight against imperialism's formula through the masses that favored the trinomial Roosevelt-Tugwell-Muñoz Marín, and on the other hand the forces that favored independence did not come together in a homogenous whole in order to take advantage of the war juncture and free Puerto Rico. So, while the Nationalists continue to resist in the prisons and in exile, the majority of independentists fell in the imperialist net and followed the trinomial. However, the strength of national spontaneity, stimulated by the different shades of libertarian inclinations that the same war imposed, and through the participation of the Soviet Union in the war, made a political echo and the Congreso Pro Independencia was organized. The formation of the Congreso Pro Independencia was evidence that the people were willing to attain independence during the war. When it called for independence the people, as always, responded generously and patriotically. And, again, the leadership failed.

The organization gathered sufficient forces to have its leadership recognized as the true representative of national unity. That new instrument for struggle had the potential to become revolutionary and of the masses, because it was not an electioneering political party as it worked outside the imperial colonialist system. Any of the two great public conventions of the Congreso could have become a Constituent Assembly of the Republic. But the leadership put the brakes on the people's liberating momentum, and subordinated the Congreso Pro Independencia to the will of the United States Congress, concentrating all its efforts on trying to obtain approval of the bill for independence presented by Senator Tydings—a ruse to deceive the people of Puerto Rico into using the liberating energies in futile discussions and polemics. As a result, the Congreso Pro Independencia disintegrated. Instead of serving as a vehicle for independence, as it could have, or at least as a foundation for an anti-imperialist front, it became instead a thoughtless instrument that helped Imperialism maintain colonialism in Puerto Rico, and later a center for a new divisiveness of independentist forces, when on October 20, 1946, a little over three years after its inception, the leadership formed another electioneering party, the Partido Independentista Puertorriqueño.

2.   Now, we will look at the other facet of the unraveling of Muñoz Marín's and his party's industrialization program.

As soon as the war ended, and the process of industrial reorganization in the United States began, the collapse of Puerto Rico's fleeting small industrial affluence started. The manifest tendency of Imperialism at the beginning of this turn resulted in a total ouster. But at the same time, there was a renewed intensification of independentist feeling. The Partido Independentista launched a wide campaign to stimulate patriotic feeling in preparation for its participation in the colonial elections of 1948. The Communist Party joined that campaign. The return of Albizu Campos in December of 1947 was another reason for revival of the emancipating struggle, bringing also to the foreground his former combativeness and renewing the anti-electoral proposition. His anti-elections proposal revealed at once the fear on the part of the imperialists and their criollo servants of this nation saving formula. All of the scoundrels of the imperialist-colonial sphere came to the fore to oppose electoral non-participation proposed by Albizu. Paradoxically, he was the target of the hatred on the part of the Partido Independentista Puertorriqueño, as were those of us who are against the electoral route as a means for independence, be they members of the *Partido Nacionalista* or not.

It is useful now to highlight the fact that the intensification of the liberating sentiment forced imperialism to raise again the banner of industrialization through Muñoz Marín and his PPD. That thinking over is what is coming through now [1949]. But it is foolish to think that it may lead to the industrial development of Puerto Rico. On the contrary, the object is to strengthen United States industry, to fill the coffers of United States industrial moguls, with Puerto Rican wealth from Puerto Rican sweat turned into wealth for its captors.

The thinking over had as its only objective to strengthen the political and economic position of colonial imperialism, by employing a few hundreds of workers in order to diminish revolutionary ferment caused by the crisis that is beginning. [47]

To make the colonial-imperialist combination work, Puerto Rican taxpayers will pay to offer the imported United States industrialists the guarantees of police, intelligence, plumbing, transportation, street lighting and electricity, in addition to the regulations necessary for the functioning of a factory.

For ten years, the United States based industries will not pay for any of the above mentioned services and will enjoy these services while the Puerto Rican taxpayers defray the costs. When each ten years are up, each industry will close the factory and take off with the enormous profits. Then, there will be a great wave on behalf of those who will lose their jobs, and, to cure that, another industry will be imported with the same tax exemptions for ten years, paid by the Puerto Rican public.

The enormous profits to be gained from such a program shall be added to the profits gained from salaries not paid. If, for example, during the first year of operations, one of these enterprises pays one million dollars in salaries, it will receive two million dollars from unpaid salaries, because cheap labor is guaranteed to these industries. The Puerto Rican worker in any of these factories will earn precisely one-third of what a

---

47 Operation Bootstrap was the industrialization program established by Muñoz Marín that forced massive flight of Puerto Ricans who were left without a livelihood.

similar worker earns in the United States. So, in ten years, and with the same average, the United States industrialist will have not paid twenty million dollars to his workers in the Island.

In short, that if Puerto Rico wants to cross expand its economic border—industrialization—it has to be disposed to crossing it with a conquering attitude, as it should be. The conquest of independence is the gaining of our opportunity for industrialization. Either we decide to conquer it, or we resign ourselves to the shameful position of being a country without industry, which is part of the ignominy of being a colony.

Here we conclude our analysis of the lie that the agrarian and industrialization policies of the Empire present to the people of Puerto Rico through Muñoz Marín and his party. And we will examine the recent acts of the United States through Luis Muñoz Marín. The first one is the statement that, "Puerto Rico is not a colony," the second is that, "nations and nationalisms have disappeared," and the third, that the election of a *criollo*—in this case Luis Muñoz Marín—as governor of Puerto Rico, has turned Puerto Rico into a "new state."

In effect, in service to United States nationalism, Muñoz has declared that Puerto Rico is no longer a colony. Muñoz's sole base for that claim is that, "Puerto Rico is not a source of raw materials for United States industries". It is a twofold lie.

Let us take for example the sugar cane industry. This truly industrialized agriculture in Puerto Rico belongs to United States financial interests. Therefore, Puerto Rico is providing sugar cane as raw material that the United States owned industry turns into sugar. We underscore, the raw material, sugar cane, is produced in Puerto Rico for an industry that does not belong to Puerto Rico and who converts into a finished product: sugar. That sugar is sold to markets in the United States and in the colony. Furthermore, that sugar produced by the United States owned mills on Puerto Rican soil leaves the Island in the merchant ships that also belong to the Unites States and United States industrialists sell it to their domestic markets and to the public in Puerto Rico.

In addition, Muñoz's statement is a lie because in terms of the economy, what characterizes a colony is not that it is a producer of raw materials alone, but that it is also a monopolistic market for the Empire. It is a bottomless basket in which the metropolis dumps its large amount of inferior products. And, as we all know, that is exactly what happens with Puerto Rico.

The most outstanding characteristic of colonial rule is the absence of sovereignty. Can anyone in his or her right mind assert that Puerto Rico is sovereign? Of course not. No one, not even Muñoz Marín. This is why his two complementary statements are equally false.

His first assertion: that nations and nationalisms have disappeared, that they are obsolete, is false because Muñoz is distorting realities, when he could have said that what is obsolete is colonialism. But nations have not disappeared. Puerto Rican nationhood has not disappeared, and as such has been referred to in an international public document—the declaration on Puerto Rico of the American States Conference in Havana, where the issue of colonialism in America was the theme—not long ago. The United States has not disappeared. On the contrary, the universal tendency is the total development of nationalities. The men of our generation have seen how, in the course of time, the Hispanic nationalities of America have grown stronger; how the Union of Soviet Socialist Republics, the Slavic nations that suffered the deformation of czarism have found definition and strength. Indonesia, India, Ireland, and the Philippines, have fully defined their national personalities, and how the Hispanic nations are posing a very desirable political agenda, a multinational agenda in the Iberian Peninsula. And further, we have seen with great pride how our own nation, in spite of the efforts of United States Imperialism and of people like Muñoz Marín is progressively strengthening a national consciousness.

Muñoz Marín is creating confusion—deliberately and with malice—regarding nations and internationalism. Without nations, internationalism cannot be, because internationalism is decent or indecent relations among nations. Muñoz Marín is not in favor of decent relations among nations. He favors the indecent relationships between subjugated nations, like Puerto Rico, and subjugating nations, like the United States. Those of us in Puerto Rico who want true and decent internationalism want independence and want Puerto Rico to join in the decent international relations with all the countries of the world.

We are not surprised that Muñoz Marín feels that Puerto Rico is a "new state". He once before was in a "new state" when he was full of budgetary ambitions. What matters, however, is not Muñoz Marín's "new state," but the palaver full of lies at the beck and call of the Empire. We will proceed to get to the bottom of this.

Muñoz's words may lead to the understanding of two things. The first is that through the election of a "native" governor, Puerto Rico has become a "state" of the union, a province of the United States. If that had been the case, Puerto Rico would not have become a new or an old state. Because the juridical essence of a state—new or old—is sovereignty. And the "states" that make up the United States are not sovereign. Once they were states, when the Thirteen Colonies became a federation to impose their independence with blood and fire upon the British Crown. But they ceased to be when the constitution through which The United States is governed was approved. If the illusion of what they once were survived for some time, it was destroyed with bullets during the Civil War of 1861. In addition, we all know that Puerto Rico has not become a province of the United States.

The understanding may be that the colonial institutions product of Congress and imposed on Puerto Rico were created with the definite idea of preparing the people of Puerto Rico for their independence. Therefore, they are endowed with and inherent liberating dynamism since their inception. Such a proposition would be equivalent to add insult to falsehood.

When—as a result of the invasion—the Empire created the colonial institutions that still exist, Puerto Rico was a nation capable of exercising sovereignty. Then as now, the Puerto Ricans could not only govern the Island, but the United States as well. Undoubtedly, if Eugenio María de Hostos had been president of the United States in 1900, the policies of that country would have been wiser and its history much more decent. It is unfortunate for that country that the people have not been able to produce a statesman of the caliber of De Hostos. But we are proud that he originated here and is guide to our Puerto Rican thought.

We say this so that the shamelessness of the insult contained in the insinuation that the colonial institutions created by the Empire's congress to dominate Puerto Rico were born of the intent to prepare the people of Puerto Rico for independence.

And after the insult, the lie. It is not true that those institutions were created with such a purpose. On the contrary, they were spawned and imposed with the purpose of destroying the Puerto Rican leadership by perverting it into collaborationism, with the purpose of progressively developing a mean, unworthy and treacherous bureaucratic machinery with the express and direct purpose of making the Puerto Rican people forget who they are, to reject their origins, disregard their own dignity, and become an immense generalized and collective prostitute. Of course then, the "dynamics" of those institutions are not conducive to a new state, but to the old "State" of Sodom and Gomorrah. And, literally, perhaps there are very few places on Earth and times in history in which so

much political prostitution has gathered together as is found
in today's governmental agencies.

If "bread and land" became what we have just said, the same
has happened to "liberty". The colony still remains a colony.
Imperialism, for its convenience, has only changed the pack
that manages and benefits from the budget.

And there is more. The new generation of budget users has
lent itself, not only to surrender Puerto Rican lands to the
military forces of the United States, without a single protest,
not even the silent protest of shame, but it has obeyed the
commands of the Empire in approving legislation that is
known as "The Gag Laws" makes illegal all and any opposition—that may cause harm to imperialism and may be really
good for the people of Puerto Rico—and entails ten years
imprisonment without bail while the accusation is sub judice.
Right now, the legislature is in the process of outlawing the
possession of arms for all with the intention of rushing into
the complete surrender of our people, and leaving them
defenseless before the government's armed bandits. A special
police force has been formed—in truth a political police
force—whose only purpose is to persecute "anti-American" in
the country. That is, all and any who with honesty and
purpose work for freedom.

To conclude this analysis of today's disgusting collaboration-
ism at the service of the United States Government, I am
reminded of something I made public with the purpose of
alerting some of those who still believe in the possibility of
attaining independence through the electoral process, and to
inform the people in general.

In September of 1939, on a Sunday afternoon we, who were
incarcerated in Atlanta, were visited by an official of the
government of the United States. According to his credentials
and his words, his visit was a mission from "his" government.
He was a Puerto Rican, residing in Washington since his law
student days. He had settled there and raised his family since

the turn of the century, and since then he worked for the State
Department or the Department of Justice. He is Pedro Capó
Rodríguez. He stated that he had instructions from "his
government" to recognize that the United States was headed
to war, and admitted that it could not face the responsibilities
of a world war without "hemispheric solidarity". And that
solidarity had but one obstacle: the "involuntary mistakes"
committed by the United States in Puerto Rico. The worst of
which, said he, was our imprisonment. The government, he
continued, recognized that we did not belong in that prison
but in Puerto Rico, where we should occupy positions for the
public good, which we deserved more than any other Puerto
Ricans. He had the authority from "his government" to assure
us that the Government was in the disposition to set us free
immediately in Puerto Rico as "safe and sound as when we
arrived in Atlanta". In addition, the Government made a
solemn promise of "guaranteeing free elections," so that the
Partido Nacionalista could win the elections of 1940, substi-
tuting the discredited General Winship with a "prestigious
figure" who would give back the government its "lost"
prestige. And the Government also promised to extend to
Puerto Rico "such a large degree of autonomy, that would be
equivalent to independence without a flag." To gain our
immediate release, we only had to declare that, "Independence
was not at issue" and ask that our friends in Latin America
stop the intense pro independence campaign on behalf of
Puerto Rico, that stirred in all of the Spanish-speaking
continent at the time.

Albizu Campos instructed me to tell Mr. Capó what I thought
[of the proposal]. My thought was that it was unworthy, that
only independence for my country could resolve the pending
business between the United States and Puerto Rico; that we
were serving our country in the outhouses of Atlanta, and that
it the United States recognized independence for Puerto Rico
in full, I, personally, would propose the dissolution of the
Partido Nacionalista and would return to my hometown of

Ciales and never leave it, even to visit a nearby town. I said other things as well. Later, Albizu Campos, commended us all while at the prison yard, and took me aside to scold me for my furious reaction to the proposal. And I was reminded of a saying original to my native mountains of Frontón: "¡*Genio y figura hasta la sepultura*!" All of us assumed the same patriotic stance. They were, besides Albizu Campos and myself: Clemente Soto Vélez, Juan Gallardo Santiago, Luis F. Velázquez, Pablo Santiago Ortiz, Julio Héctor Velázquez, and Erasmo Velázquez.

The government's envoy left with great courtesy while he warned us that his mission began in Atlanta but would not end there. He would travel to Puerto Rico to meet with other leaders. And so he did. He met with Muñoz Marín, and independence "was not at issue".

Small-minded beggars! Who were satisfied with the miserly leftovers from starving, ragged, and jailed men who were thousands of miles away from their country. And they have not had the courage to demand what they were promised in exchange for their puny souls. They have been content with much less. In order not to think, they unscrew their heads, and to show that they do not have hearts, they become more despicable every day, not only in the eyes of the people, but in the eyes of their masters who despise them as much as they use them!

11

ELECTIONS AND BOYCOTT

In a previous chapter we explained how imperialism, having taken our national territory by force of arms, used the economic misery they created with the currency exchange to pit Puerto Ricans against one another. And the base for this division in a fratricidal electoral struggle was the bankruptcy of our economy, all set up by the empire. There are other factors, as well, related to achieving the catastrophe. [But in this Chapter], we will point to one of the greatest importance.

For many years, apologists for parliamentary democracy had been pushing in Puerto Rico the blind virtues of the United States electoral system. The people of Puerto Rico were in need of and aspired to, as did the rest of the people in Latin American, the establishment of an all-encompassing electoral system. The United States government found a small source of favorable opinion for the systematization of the electoral process in the island. But the people, disoriented by their leaders, could not see—unfortunately—that its historical future was at the mercy of a crap game with loaded dice that spelled "colony" every time they were thrown. Pulled by its pseudo leaders to run after an illusory and cruel democratic mirage, the country was tricked into a headfirst plunge toward elections with the same suicidal momentum that a bull throws itself at the bullfighter's sword. But the pillar of parliamentary democracy is national sovereignty, and without the second, the first cannot exist.

The United States won a game of long-term consequences. The electoral system, founded by them to ensure their occupation of Puerto Rico is still in place, so successfully that a few months ago [48] a small group of Puerto Ricans, spell-bound by the deceit that it was putting up a good fight for independence, took to the polls a political party [for independence]. The monetary profits gained by imperialism every time that our people–unheeding the voice of our historical past, our experience, and

---

48 The time is 1949.

patriotism—vote in colonial elections every four years, as ordained by Congress, amount to billions of dollars. We will not delve into those statistics now. Instead, we will point to the enormous political gains obtained by Imperialism whenever Puerto Ricans go to the colonial polls.

1. The motto for any empire to keep its grip on a people is always the same: Divide and conquer. By establishing the electoral struggle the United States created divisions among the Puerto Ricans and will keep them divided until we break their scheme by uniting to combat it outside the electoral machine. Elections are the best weapon of political domination. By participating in elections, Puerto Ricans accept United States' domination of their country.

2. The Government of the United States knows that international moral conscience and the juridical knowledge are well aware that it seized Puerto Rico forcefully and violently; and it keeps it under colonial submission through organized force and violence by using its armed forces to control the island's economy. The Government of the United States also knows that it has no right to govern Puerto Rico. It is entirely responsible for this act of imperialistic imposition. But wanting to preserve prestige within the international community, it wishes to make Puerto Ricans responsible for their own slavery. When islanders participate in elections, they give the United States the argument to claim that the Puerto Ricans are enslaved by choice.

3. Because the empire knows this and wants to leave no doubt with regard to the Puerto Ricans' consent to being governed by it, it has determined that the people of the Island of Puerto Rico ratify their colonial status at the polls every four years, and with that, authorize the United States to continue governing Puerto Rico.

4. As citizenship is the mark of nationality, through congressional law, the United States imposed on the Puerto Ricans, a colonial—Yankee citizenship in order to be rid of Puerto

Rican citizenship, and thus accept the "yankeezation" of the islanders. When Puerto Ricans vote, obeying a law from Congress, they do so as Yankees and not as Puerto Ricans. The empire's gain from this is that the voters deny their Puerto Rican citizenship, and accept United States citizenship.

5.   In order to govern Puerto Rico, the empire created, through congressional law, a corporation known as "The People of Puerto Rico". That corporation has nothing to do with the real people of Puerto Rico. It has nothing to do with those people who are born, sing and suffer, struggle and never die. That juridical entity, created by the Congress of the United States, is a United States corporation. It set the by-laws that created the imperial-colonial institutions needed to maintain Puerto Rico enslaved. But the key institution—without which all the others would collapse—is electoral participation. Through elections in Puerto Rico imperialism nurtures the divisions of Puerto Ricans into political parties that struggle for the [colonial] budget. This ensures domination, because as we all know, the intention of every empire is to divide and conquer. Through elections, the empire renews its energies every four years to keep its despotic yoke around Puerto Rico. Those new energies are provided by the people of Puerto Rico when they participate in the electoral process. As the empire obtains the people's acquiescence to taking on the responsibility for its own colonial domination, the international face of the United States is wiped clean, and its international political power is strengthened, not only over the island-nation, but over the Latin American countries and the other peoples of the world that are chained to world imperialism, headed by the United States.

Through participation at the polls, the people of Puerto Rico appear as reneging their natural citizenship and agreeing to United States citizenship, thus rejecting their Puerto Rican nationality. By participating in colonial elections, Puerto Ricans are granting to the United States the "right" to occupy

their island and treat its people and resources in a despotic
manner. Elections in Puerto Rico are the key to political
domination on the part of the empire, the Gordian knot
paralyzing our destiny, and which we will destroy in one fell
swoop.

6.   To all this must be added the net gain that the empire
      obtains from the people or Puerto Rico's concurrence to the
      polls, contained in the absolute uselessness of the elections
      for Puerto Rico. That means that the elections are the key
      imperialist-colonial institution in Puerto Rico, and because
      the imperialist-colonial institutions have been created by
      Congress, it is that body that holds political power over
      Puerto Rico and not the islanders. Therefore, the attainment
      of political power over Puerto Rico is never in contest when
      elections are held in the Island under those circumstances.
      This proves the absolute uselessness, the vacuous foolishness
      of going to the polls and voting in colonial elections, where
      the electorate is vying for political power that is held very far
      away in Washington. That is why, when Puerto Ricans go to
      the colonial rigged polls, in pursuit of their ideals, they are
      playing the painful and ridiculous role of the donkey pulling
      the wheel: moving in circles, going nowhere.

      But from this same uselessness of the elections for the Puerto
      Ricans the empire attains yet another gain of singular impor-
      tance. It is that the campaigning period and the elections serve
      to defuse the emotional energies of the people, discharging
      them through the electoral wasteland into the garbage dump
      of history; frustrated, useless, and causing alienation of the
      Puerto Rican spirit. Wasted also with the elections are our
      physical energies and our economic resources. Imperialism is
      thus ensured of its position of power, vigorous and clean
      looking, at a time when all the imaginative fighting spirit of
      our people could have threatened its power in the Island.
      Instead, it is discharged into nothingness.

We have sketched the gains received by the empire from colonial elections. Now, we will point to at least two false positions assumed by the Puerto Ricans, who justify their participation in them.

1. We must, some say, go to vote although we know that it is not the best option, because if we abstain from voting the government will be taken over by the most unpatriotic and reactionary elements in the country and by Yankees, while the people would not have the relative protection of the patriotic and progressive element participating in the colonial government.

    The falsehood of this statement stands out in view of the results of the latest elections. [49] That is a colonized, reformist, debasing position; absurd and criminal. It is founded on the absolute lack of knowledge of the capabilities and the revolutionary strength of the Puerto Rican people, and of its international potential. It is a position based upon contempt for the people of Puerto Rico, beginning with the premise that we must be content with the crumbs the empire is willing to give us and we should make the best of it. That way of thinking leads to permanent slavery, preached and sustained by all the criollo reformists, led today by Luis Muñoz Marín and his followers. Historical experience shows us that—just as the examination of history proves it—that such a position will lead to the destruction of our possibilities [as a nation] and invites us to destroy Puerto Rican Nationhood. The same as when in 1897, Muñoz Rivera and the Autonomists pushed us into the frustration of our revolutionary process of the nineteenth century and into the degradation of United States occupation. The tragedy for the country is that the people accepted the guidance of that reformist position, from Celis Aguilera and Pedro Gerónimo Goyco to Luis Muñoz Marín. This history is clearly written on the Puerto Rican faces and

---

49 Elections of 1948

bears the signature of the colonial chains that are still binding us.

2. Another false position that some Puerto Ricans take regarding the participation in elections is that we need to vote because we cannot opt for revolution. That is a defeatist position founded in the blind distrust of the revolutionary capability of the people, in the lack of faith in the masses, in confusing the momentary triumph of the imperialist-colonial propaganda with the infinite, incommensurable potential for revolution that the people of Puerto Rico possess.

To hold on to that false position, its supporters resort to a historic argument that does not have antecedents in truth. They say that Puerto Rican independence can be obtained through peaceful means (that is, elections), in "peace and harmony" with the people of the United States (that is with the consent of the empire). Therefore, they argue, that any revolutionary proposition as solution to the problem is unnecessary and even harmful to the possibility of independence.

This is the first falsehood of that thesis. When the United States' fleet bombarded our capital by surprise attack in May of 1898, we had not done any violence against the United States government. Nor was there a justification when they entered through Guánica, shooting. The subjugation of our country by force of arms, the sequestration of our sovereignty, the robbery they committed with the imposition of the currency exchange that led to the destruction of our economy, the threat to our language and culture, are all violent acts against us committed by the United States. The incarceration of the Puerto Rican journalists immediately following the invasion, the incitement to civil war, first between *federales* and *republicanos*, then between *republicanos* and *unionistas*, and later of employers and police against workers during the growing phase of the Partido Socialista.

The official terrorism during the Reilly and Winship regimes, are proof that it is the empire who resorts to violence, assassinations, massacres, imprisonment and exile whenever Puerto Ricans initiate a new phase of struggle in defense of their Homeland. With these eloquent testimonies extracted from the history of our land under submission to imperialism, we highlight the truth that the rapacious and aggressive nature of the United States responds with violence to the demands for freedom of the Puerto Rican people.

Therefore, those Puerto Ricans who propose liberating Puerto Rico through "peaceful means" are very mistaken. Because in the long run, either they will knuckle under the colonial power or become its lackeys. Or violent repression will overrun them and force them to disband. Because the spirit of their followers who dream of a "peaceful conquest" of independence will not be up to fighting the enemy, nor will they have the resources to do so; and mustering inner strength, they will take a serious and correct position in the revolutionary camp, ending brainlessly where they should have been conscientiously from the beginning.

These individuals who believe in the "peaceful" camp, in "peace and harmony" so that, in the not so far future, they may become useful to their country; so that they may, if they wish, help liberate it, must begin by erasing from their minds the illusions of gaining independence through words and paperwork, "peaceful", electoral, diplomatic tactics, that are exclusively legalistic and essentially Reformist. That amounts to already experienced historical failure and, in addition, our leading political consciousness has matured beyond that.

Another argument posed by those same people, also erroneous because it is a contradiction, is the notion of "transforming the colonial institutions into instruments for independence." This takes for granted that there is a steadfast and honest pro-independence political party that goes to the colonial elections "in peace and harmony," and transforms the enslaving elections, by taking over the colonial administrative machine and budget, and uses them to wage political struggle against the empire.

Those who propose that are deluding themselves completely with regard to the nature of imperialism (which we have already described), and forget that in voting they do not do so as Puerto Ricans, but as citizens of the United States. To vote they had to sign a sworn statement in which they affirmed faithfulness and loyalty as United States citizens; in which case the empire would not even have to resort to force of arms to eliminate that first liberating attempt. For, operating within the same legalistic framework designed by the United States and accepted by these "liberators," a mere trial for perjury would suffice to land them in prison.

But supporting the empire allowed them to win at the polls and not be incarcerated for perjury; and neither Washington's Supreme Court, nor Congress, nor the president intervened by issuing a decision, a resolution, or a decree nullifying the elections (as they can, within the imperialist-colonialist framework that these "liberators" want to make use of). The framework itself would operate as a straight jacket. Accepting such a proposal is impossible because it is based on a false historical precedent.

To validate their proposal, these people resort to two known historical events. But when both processes are examined, we shall see that they were not equal to the situation in Puerto Rico. Those who support this position assert that the Latin American countries were born of such a process in the early nineteenth century.

It is true that the Hispano American peoples employed the colonial institutions established by the viceroyalties and the captaincies-general to wage political struggles for independence; and later freed them from the Spanish empire. But such a happy event does not apply to Puerto Rico's present situation.

When the Hispano Americans began to employ the colonial institutions to fight politically against the Spanish regime, they did not have to enter into a previous political struggle wielding the independence banner in order to first gain it and then turn it against the empire. They were in the struggle because of concessions made by the Crown. This bears no resemblance to the position taken by the group who would have to declare themselves for independence and then scurry into gaining posts in the colonial government while at the same time proclaiming far and wide that they will use these posts to fight the empire. It is ridiculous not to expect that such would be the situation of this group, given their proposal.

In the end, it was not the lobbyists who freed our America with speeches and paperwork, but the courageous revolutionaries who gave up on the lobbyists and exchanged shots with the Spanish troops, after raising the revolutionary consciousness of the people.

Another example used as historical example for the electoral theory of using "peaceful and legal means," "in peace and harmony" and "law and order" is the Philippines. Those who support that theory and claim to defend independence say that the Philippinos did not obtain their independence by fighting against the United States, but in the political arena, peacefully, "In peace and harmony". That by means of separatist political parties the Philippinos won elections, made use of the colonial institutions and budget to fight for their independence. And thus the decent, paternalistic, democratic, United States imperialism did not hesitate to recognize independence for the Philippines.

Nothing could be further from the truth. That is nothing but a tale promoted by the State Department of the United States government. No Puerto Rican patriot should advocate for it. The history of Philippine independence is quite different and cannot be used as historical example to propose independence for the island.

When the United States landed in the Philippines, an armed struggle was taking place to free the archipelago from Spanish clutches. When the Philippino fighters realized that the intentions of the invaders were to take the place of the Spaniards, they fought them with weapons. Concerned with the international prestige that this struggle with the Philippinos would cost and, on the Philippine side, the fact that their ammunitions supplies were low, the United States proposed, and the Philippinos were forced to accept, the public recognition by the United States that the Philippines had the right to become an independent and sovereign nation. A formal commitment on the part of the government of the United States was obtained, to recognize Philippino freedom and to help them on the road to independence. That is the meaning of Aguinaldo's [50] surrender.

But in Puerto Rico, at the end of the nineteenth century, what happened in the Philippines did not occur. Instead, the reformists led by Muñoz Rivera, undermined the revolutionary camp, paving the way for

---

50 General Emilio Aguinaldo was the first president of the Philippine government formed to fight the occupying United States forces in 1898.

the new masters. Resulting in no revolt. Muñoz Rivera did not speak the patriotic and fiery language that filled the hearts of the Philippinos and the United States was not forced to make the same promise to the Puerto Ricans. This explains the impudence and cynicism with which they state that, "The United States has not made promises to Puerto Rico that it has not fulfilled."

But after making that commitment to the Philippinos, the United States did all it could to not have to keep its promise. Instead of helping them to gain independence, it penetrated its economy and corrupted every corruptible national to turn him against his country. Nevertheless, the leadership in general remained alert and the people steadfastly patriotic. And they did not let those leaders who might falter loose track of the goal of independence.

So it was not out of desire or goodness, or decency, that in 1936, the United States Congress approved the law that created the Commonwealth of the Philippines as a transitional step toward independence, ten years hence. The transitional regime, the cruel ten-year wait imposed on the Philippinos, was achieved through penetration of the economy and of the leadership, but was nevertheless concessions made to the Philippino people who had demanded loudly and clearly with patriotic impatience for liberty.

The great crisis of capitalism in the United States had deep repercussions on the Philippines, and bred a revolutionary ferment that threatened imperialism as well as the native nouveau riche who got fat while the workers and peasants went hungry. Dangerous rumblings were heard in the hills of Luzón and Mindanao. The people sought a brilliant mind like Rizal's, [51] and the strong arm of Aguinaldo, and in May 1935, the United States drowned in blood a patriotic insurrection.

Meanwhile, Hirohito's [Japanese] empire loomed with its warships on the horizon. Thus, the political leadership's struggle, the ferment of revolutionary ebullience and the threat of insurrection coupled with the fear of international disgrace, forced the United States to set the date for the establishment of the Philippine Republic.

---

51 José Rizal, physician and writer, executed by the Spanish colonizers as a revolutionary. While he is considered among the earliest of Phillippine patriots, his writing was not in any of the dialects native to the Philippines, but in Spanish.

After all that, and after the people paid with amazing heroism and an enormous price in blood for their independence by joining the United States in the fight against Japan—they did not, as some fools believe, fight to save "American Democracy," but to guarantee their own independence—we still remember the hypocrisy with which the imperialists began to probe Philippine public opinion to see if the recognition of independence could be postponed. It took all that struggle, heroism and bloodshed for the United States to recognize the independence that the Philippines now enjoy! They earned it with arms, not passively, not with "law and order" nor "through peace and harmony."

In addition, the Philippine situation is not comparable with Puerto Rico's in the historical development that took place in that archipelago following Aguinaldo's insurrectional prologue.

In 1936, when the Philippinos won the setting of a date for their independence, Puerto Rico was struggling heroically for its own. And that same year the "peaceful" independentists who push "peace and harmony" frustrated the liberating process with their betrayal of the revolutionary cause at the *Asamblea Liberal* in Yauco, and by dividing the separatist forces in that year's elections; once again surrendering the country to "law and order" (in truth, to the Empire's political domination and economic exploitation).

The Puerto Ricans need peace and harmony to make independence possible. But it is the inner peace and harmony that assures a capable revolutionary mandate that emanates from the action of the masses. And they need to rule their lives forever in law and order, but in the lawfulness of attained independence, and with the order that would be obtained by triumphant revolution. That must be realized with the clearest understanding that no state of liberty is infinitely attainable. Such conditions of Puerto Rican well being, of achieved independence and possibility of functioning for the Puerto Ricans as constant achievers of freedom, presuppose, necessarily, the previous destruction of the "law and order" that now exist and are in truth at the service of an enslaving and exploitative imperialism.

The reality is that elections keep us enslaved and the experience that our country has lived because of them, point to the advisability of abandoning the polls and resorting instead to non participation and boycott, as a tactic of political struggle for independence. Once the independence movement reaches the decision to boycott colonial elections, the means to organize, the links that lead progressively to the phases of struggle, and the resolution of problems, will flow as we see the lowering forever of the imperialist flag and the raising of the triumphant flag of our beloved Homeland.

Instead of the overwhelming negativity that colonial elections mean for us, we present the indisputable positivity of their boycott.

1. Elections divide Puerto Ricans and only benefit the empire. The more divided, the greater the harm for the Island and the greater benefit for the United States. Non-participation and boycott is in and of itself so strong and clear that from the start it will lead to unity devoid of budget ambitions, false glory, and ridiculous posturing. It will ensure for the initial groupings a power of cohesion and struggle that the elections-pushing groups cannot equal. Employing electoral non participation and boycott assures the masses a true and strong leadership, proven in the struggle by its honesty, capacity for dedication, and self-sacrifice for the good of all, through proven strength of character and the necessary courage to face the common enemy.

    A divided people have never united just on words. The newspaper article, the public speech, the flyer, the radio broadcast are all valuable tools that help widen the struggle. But the electoral proposal reduces them all, by necessity and in a fundamental way, to instruments of propaganda. Propaganda alone is not sufficient to liberate a country or to unite its people. Moreover, the anti-electoral proposal adds immediately the very valuable element of agitation. Sustained agitation inevitably leads to action. And action unites disunited peoples. We assert that electoral participation in Puerto Rico is not even political action; it is colonial inaction, inability to be rid of the established patterns imposed by the enemy. To propose, then, an anti-electoral tactic, produces among its followers a certain degree of unity, cohesion, empowerment to strive for higher-minded struggles. It makes the empowerment more widespread when the people discard a false and hesitant leadership, in order to take possession of an instrument that begets strong, dedicated, self-sacrificing leadership, with character and courage to struggle and suffer and face the enemy for the attainment of the common good.

In addition, the anti-electoral proposal guarantees for the people a leadership of superior intellect, because contrary to the mentality of the electioneering leadership, the first requires the freedom of spirit that enables it to think of the Homeland as functioning without colonial shackles; an intellect capable of thinking of its country as already liberated. That freedom, that emancipation of the national mind will begin with the refusal to participate in elections. Will give it life and reach the peak of struggle and full national maturity when independence is achieved.

2.   To reject electoral participation puts in the hands of the government of the United States, without a doubt, Puerto Rico's colonial status. When collaboration blessed by elections is paralyzed, the United States' international prestige will be damaged. Its hypocritical "democracy" will be exposed for what it is; and for the first time that country will have to assume responsibility before the Puerto Ricans and the world.

3.   In rejecting elections, the islanders will reject the colony, halt its machinery and embark on the road to independence.

4.   By refusing to participate in the elections Puerto Ricans will reject the humiliating citizenship imposed by the United States, reaffirm Puerto Rican citizenship and with that also reaffirm the Nationhood and prove false the so much touted "Americanization" of Puerto Rico.

5.   By refusing to participate in the elections the whole nation of Puerto Ricans will also reject the false allegation that Congress is the depository of our destiny and political power, and reaffirm that they are the only masters of their destiny and the sole source of political power in Puerto Rico. That

will ensure sovereignty; proclaim a sovereign act, weaken imperial power; and will put our country in the liberating mode, because it would weaken despotic imperialism headed by the United States in the world.

6. Faced with elections rendered useless by the refusal to participate and the boycott of elections, the energies of all Puerto Ricans would be channeled into national consciousness of a revolutionary nature, and transformed it into the force of our history and of the history of humanity, putting them at the service of three quarters of the world's population who suffers despotic rules from the world chain of imperialism headed by the United States. Puerto Rico would be the anti-imperialist vanguard in the Americas, and all of Latin America would be thankful to us for our struggle. The forces that propel history will have put us in that position and we will honor that placement. We owe ourselves the inescapable duty of freeing us from the imperial yoke imposed by the United States. Thus we would help our sister nations in Latin America to rid themselves completely of the domination from monopolistic capital controlled by the United States, which shrinks their international activities and damages their historical path. Electoral boycott would guarantee our independence and with that we would raise the political level of the struggle in all of Latin America. Our revolutionary struggle for independence would give life, through our example, to the Latin American peoples, pushing them to a deeper anti-imperialist fight. With anti-imperialist fight in all of Latin America we will weaken the common enemy, and help to finally eliminate imperialism and colonialism in the world; thus helping to the organization of a truly free universal society. That is the true ideal of man on earth. Such were the ideals of the Founders of our Homeland and of our America: Betances, Hostos, Bolívar, Martí, Artigas and Morazán. These are the same ideals contained in the notion of confederating the Antilles and uniting Latin America.

But before we can begin all this glorious plan of historic action, we must remember that the first step is freeing the people's spirit. That freedom will begin by freeing ourselves from the enslaving inertia of the elections.

We must get ready, right now, to boycott the elections!

12

MILITARY SERVICE

Until 1868, Puerto Ricans served as volunteers in the *criolla* militias organized in our country by the Spanish Empire. After the Lares Revolt, the militias were eliminated. This has a deep historical meaning and no one can deny the repercussions of their dissolution, following the insurrection.

Through the centuries of formation of Puerto Rican nationhood—before the early nineteenth century—the establishment of the militias and the volunteer service in them were a way of organizing the country's will. That was the positive side, and as such, during the latter part of the seventeenth, through the eighteenth, and in the early nineteenth centuries, the militias were a decisive factor to the formation of the nationhood because the Puerto Rican will, organized within the militias ensured definitively the Hispanic values of Puerto Rican society, making it what it is today: a Latin American nation. This is the historical meaning of our defensive forces against French, Dutch and English attacks commanded in San Juan by Amézquita, by Ramírez de Arellano in San Germán, Correa in Arecibo, Caballero in Loíza, and Henríquez, and Leguillou in Vieques.

But changes occurred in the first ten years of the nineteenth century. "By the first decade of the nineteenth century, Puerto Rico was not the wild territory that O'Reilly described in 1765." [52] As the country matured, the meaning of the militias—for the Puerto Ricans—changed. That change was evidenced when, in 1810, the people displayed one of the first manifestations of a sense of nationhood.

[One hundred ninety] [53] years ago—1810—[continental] America ceased to belong to Spain. A Royal Commissioner, Don Antonio Ignacio de Cortarrabia, arrived to our shores. The Crown had entrusted him with

---

52 Salvador Brau, *Historia de Puerto Rico*, D. Appleton, New York, 1904.
53 Translator's update. The original text said: "One hundred thirty nine..."

directing from San Juan the war against the *Libertadores de Venezuela.* This aristocrat had the bad idea of incorporating the Puerto Rican militias to the troops that were to invade the sister nation. The rumor about his plan spread like wildfire and a poster—still, well remembered—let him know in no uncertain terms that the Puerto Rican people "will never allow that a single militia man be taken to fight against his brothers in Caracas." The outrage was such that the Royal Commissioner had to give up the plan and—to appease the uproar—free three Venezuelan deputies that were incarcerated in El Morro Castle.

Fifty-four years later, the Spanish Empire tried again to use Puerto Rican militias. Unexpectedly, a battalion was taken to Santo Domingo. The sister peninsula was aflame with glorious restorative war. Again, an angry Boricua manifesto: "Comrades, how much longer will we allow the Spanish despots to take advantage of our inaction?" The greater number of those militiamen taken to Dominican shores by surprise and deception, crossed over to the nationalist ranks, as soon as they landed, the minority chose desertion or suicide to avoid fighting against their Dominican brothers.

That question: "How much longer will we allow the Spanish despots to take advantage of our inaction?" was born of history, blood and shame. Four years later Puerto Rico gave its response with the insurrection at Lares.

Devigne, mayor of Cabo Rojo in 1868, knew well the political and social climate of the country in September of that year. In his memoirs, when referring to the account of the Lares Revolt made by the Spaniard Pérez Moris, he said that, "The historian most attentive to detail had to refrain from revealing many and important names." Imperial convenience so ordained it. The mayor's statement is proof of the truth of Balances' assertion that "in 1868 the country was ready." [54] The hidden meaning of the mayor's statement is that the militiamen who rebelled against the Royal Commissioner [in 1810], and later in 1864—four years before the Lares Revolution—went to the Dominican ranks, deserted or even chose suicide to avoid fighting on the side of the Spanish Empire, incited to

---

54 Guzmán Rodríguez, *Epistolario de Betances Correspondencia diplomática*: Betances. Tomo II. Academia Cubana de la Historia.

rebellion in a public manifesto were going to fulfill the new destiny that they should have in the nineteenth century: to make up the essential core of the Liberating Army. The reformists that couched their treason in the failure of the Lares Revolution—betrayed and forced to act prematurely—frustrated the liberating purpose of the militiamen. From 1868 onward, no Puerto Rican could serve with dignity in the regular or irregular ranks of the Spanish Army. The Crown understood that and dissolved the militias.

Not withstanding the events just described, Spain never imposed military service on its colonies. The militias were made up of volunteers whose function was exclusively to defend the country. If there was the abusive intention to use them for extraordinary ends, the incident did not go beyond intent. The will of the Puerto Ricans prevented it.

In the history of the world there is no other precedent of an empire conscripting the inhabitants of its colonies by force to fight its wars. That, "Honor," that, "privilege," that precedent have only been a part of the history of United States' despotism in Puerto Rico. That imperialistic aggregate—despicable and infamous—imposed compulsory military service for Puerto Ricans in 1917 during the presidency of Woodrow Wilson. While Puerto Rican manhood was in the Panamanian [training] camps, Wilson and his government sullied the island with the Jones Law. Again, in 1939, United States tyranny headed by Franklin Delano Roosevelt, imposed compulsory military service for Puerto Rican men.

Having broken the continuity of historic experience, taken by surprise and herded by the propaganda, Puerto Rico did not respond in 1917 with sufficient energy. The Empire prepared a plan for national collaboration that had broken our leadership, and for 14 years the country had been weakened. Nevertheless, a group of good men rejected the imposition of the colonial-imperialistic citizenship, and a handful of courageous men refused to serve.

The imposition of military conscription fell upon Puerto Rico in 1939 after four years of fierce official terrorism. The Nationalist leadership was incarcerated in Atlanta, and had rejected the offer of release and of administering the colony in exchange for giving up independence. In the Island, persecution, cruel siege and merciless bullets had reduced the resistance to a symbolic number.

But even so, the interim leadership and the best of the ranks of the Nationalist Party kept heart. Under the interim leadership, first of Ramón Medina Ramírez and later of Julio Santiago, called for resistance, both boards were thrown into federal prisons in the United States. The best of them stood up to be counted. Not much more could be expected after the country had been subjected to such cruel repression.

Once more, United States imperialism resumed its dream of attaining world domination. Having participated in two European wars that, according to plan served its own preparatory ends for world domination, having strengthened its industrial machinery, accustomed its people to take part in European conflicts, eliminated rivals, is now setting the stage for a third world war: the one that will define the "American Century". The war that will ensure the entire world as its colony at the disposal of United States industries, protected by its armed forces.

Since [1948] a new law of obligatory military service for Puerto Rican youth is in effect. To date, young men, all members of the *Partido Nacionalista*, have been imprisoned and sentenced to exile and incarceration for refusing to serve in the ranks on their country's enemy.

Undoubtedly, the country is not understanding well the transcendental importance of resisting conscription. To serve in the armed forces of the country that unlawfully holds the Homeland's sovereignty is, in anyplace in the world, the lowest form of treason. It is evident that the young men who have gone to serve under the United States flag do not understand that. Every Puerto Rican who has understood the meaning of serving in the United States armed forces preferred prison and exile to wallowing in the dung hill of treason. But there are those who have done it not realizing the meaning of their acts. Let us then explain what it means for Puerto Ricans to serve in the armed forces of the United States.

When a Puerto Rican agrees to join the United States military he is swearing loyalty to the death to that country's flag. He is agreeing to kill or be killed for that flag. He is agreeing to be killed by men from other countries who have not declared war against his country, nor his family, nor him personally. He accepts to be killed by or to kill human beings from other countries who have in no way insulted his country, nor his family, nor himself, in defense of the government that unlawfully holds the sovereignty of his Homeland and with that act offends his family's honor and his own dignity. In so doing, he is affirming with his own life, with his decision to kill or be killed for the United States flag in a more profound way than the person who serves that country's flag in civilian government, or the individual who employs the enslaving vote—the one that gives the United States the right to keep Puerto Rico under colonial rule. As if that were not enough, he accepts the duty of murdering all Puerto Ricans whenever his Yankee chiefs order it. So any Puerto Rican who has worn or is now wearing the uniform of the United States armed forces is a potential murderer of his countrymen.

As all acts of human beings in their respective countries, military service on behalf of the United States has harmful international consequences. The islanders who serve in those armed forces, and the ones who passively accept it leave an open door to horrific danger of a monstrous war, make us a magnet for the horrors of bombings, expose the Homeland to extinction. Such power has the absence of conscientiousness.

But those of us who fight against military service for the Puerto Ricans in the armed forces of the United States are denying the [invader] the alleged right to govern us and deny for the whole world to see that we the Puerto Ricans have lost collective shame, supposedly when willing to serve in the ranks of those who have sequestered our sovereignty. Of course it is known abroad—as we know—that the great majority of Puerto Ricans are forcefully inducted. It is therefore known that most of us have not lost our sense of shame. But it would be healthier and much more honorable to refuse outright to serve the master and take the consequences. And that is also well known abroad. And there, as well as here, each individual is appreciated for his true worth; and each person is worthy for his actions.

Those of us who fight against military service in the armed forces of the United States are, in addition, very much aware of its significance for our country as an international factor and as strength before the world.

We stated before that the United States is preparing for a new war through which it seeks to dominate the world. Since the murderous act of Hiroshima ended the Second World War, very profound changes have taken place in the political structure of the United States. Imperialist United States has taken the place of Nazi Germany as the leader of the savage hordes, enslavers of countries and exploiters of humanity. The strength of its monopolies has shifted the political leadership of the United States from the traditional political parties— which still operate publicly as a front—to a new secret party, already known, already seen in public and whose leaders are also known. No one mentions it because it is taboo, and who dares name it in public will land in prison or will be killed. It is the Militarist Party, whose best-known leader and whose influence terrifies many is ex-colonial governor of Puerto Rico, Admiral William D. Leahy.

To gain the favor of the military leadership for their own particular interests, the monopolies and the combinations of monopolies have placed more than one hundred high-ranking officers of the armed forces in high administrative positions throughout the world.

Puerto Ricans who serve in the United States armed forces and the Puerto Ricans who do not fight against compulsory military service in Puerto Rico are directly or indirectly serving the United States in its efforts to subjugate the world including, of course, the permanent domination of Puerto Rico.

This cooperation of the islanders in the universal imperialist ends of the United States is even more patent when looked at from the Hispano American perspective. The military occupation of Puerto Rico has always served the United States to threaten all of Latin America. As the Island grows historically, and Latin America grows accordingly the United States reinforces its military strength in Puerto Rico by building enormous bases. The direct imperialist purpose of these displays of force is obvious. It is to cause fear in the hearts of all Latin Americans, from the Puerto Ricans on down to the Argentineans. The purpose of the huge amphibian maneuvers carried out in Vieques a year ago [55] was to dramatize the putting out of a Puerto Rican insurrection for independence.

The Yankees must not be too pleased with the Puerto Ricans. There are fearful people in any country. But if the main objective was to frighten the liberation movement, the results were absolutely the contrary. The numbers of Puerto Ricans who put our independence before their lives have increased in quality and quantity, since that day in

---

55 The island of Vieques was taken by the United States Navy in 1941.

October of 1935 [56] when the empire tested our will to fight and we did not fail our Homeland.

Equally significant is an event that occurred a few months ago, when a strike shook the monopolistic interests of the United States in Bolivia. Four enormous United States warplanes were sent in a hurry from the base at Punta Borinquen in the northeast of Puerto Rico, to put down the strike in Bolivia.

Can it now be understood the importance for the United States of the Puerto Ricans in the armed forces and of those who do not fight against their compulsory conscription in terms of the subjugation of all of Latin America? Is it then logical that Puerto Ricans who proclaim to be defenders of our independence and even ardent Hispanoamericanists should remain silent and bow their heads in servility at the imperialistic command that forces Puerto Ricans to join their armed forces to turn them into the assassins of their own countrymen, and to be a part of the blackmailing forces against our larger homeland: the community of Hispano American countries?

Neither the empire, nor the vilest treason, nor the worst reformism has contradicted our position against compulsory conscription with the arbitrary sophism that some political groups have been employing lately. What are the origins of their arguments? Let us see how the worst kind of blindness is exercised. What I have heard—with more horror than surprise—from a young Puerto Rican who was forced to join the United States armed forces. He stated that he would be serving better the cause of independence in the United States army than in prison. To that statement I will limit my reply to the following: Who can be counted upon as defender of independence for the Homeland? The one who chose to wear the Yankee uniform, or the one who proved his patriotism in the hell of a United States prison? Only the distortion of moral reality can answer that unfavorably about the youth who chose to resist conscription.

After 1868, no self respecting Puerto Rican could serve with patriotism in the army of the Spanish King. Presently, there is not even a possible dignification of islanders who serve in the armed forces of the United States. The cruel break with the Puerto Rico's reality, the

---

56 Riggs's execution was in response to the Río Piedras Massacre.

disinformation that the country receives in that respect, the example of the Puerto Ricans who have affirmed that disorientation with their conduct, makes it impossible for all to remain blind, excepting those who have chosen not to see because of personal convenience.

13

INDEPENDENCE AND CLASS STRUGGLE

In a palatial home in Villa Caparra, [57] a well to do gentleman reads—pleased with himself while sitting on a cushy chair—a magazine from the United States. He is fortyish, well perfumed and dressed, with the typical self-assurance of such men to whom life has been generous. Next to him, on a dainty table, a respectful manservant has placed a drink.

Far away, sugar cane plantation workers have toiled for him under deplorable conditions. His bank account is large, so is his credit. He owns an apartment in New York, and when a friend comes to visit he greets him happily with: "*Hola comín. ¿Qué tal de uiquén?*" [58] And he introduces his son "Junior" to this fop from the University of Puerto Rico.

The wife—elegantly dressed—joins the scene. There is an exchange of pleasantries. Then, Bayamón sends upon the aristocratic mansion its daily shower. Pointing to the glass windows the beauty says: "*Nene ciérrate el uindo que se moja la fornitura.*" [59]

Naturally, the dweller of that mansion is a capitalist and has his own vision of Puerto Rico and its problems. It would be foolish to think that there are none others like him in the island. On the contrary, all of the members of his class have a common understanding of what the island and its problems are. They are all part of the bourgeoisie. They understand Puerto Rico from the point of view of their class, but are subservient and slave to the great bourgeoisie of the United States. They are its instruments, and have a slave owner understanding of Puerto Rico and its problems. Therefore, that class is colonialist and reactionary, defends the status quo, hates independence and despises the masses.

---

57 Wealthy suburb in the outskirts of San Juan.
58 "Hello, come in. How was your weekend?"
59 "Darling, close the window because the furniture is getting wet."

Our tour of the island takes us to a comfortable, although modest, home on the outskirts of the metropolitan area. The owner has a regular annual income. He works a lot and is able to pay a few employees. His domestic bliss is supported by his work as an effective representative of a United States' firm. He is a businessman whose possessions are the fruit of his labor. He has not had to climb up from the ranks of the working class, because his father, with sacrifice, put him through business school. His student days gave him a taste of books and, sometimes, reads literature. Books and experience have taught him that his personal, intimate wish that he tells no one about: being one of the rich blue-blooded, is unattainable. His path upward is blocked by the alliance between the *criolla* bourgeoisie at the beck and call of the bourgeoisie from the United States. Oh, that great industry that he has in mind! But the United States' "dumping" in the island would destroy it! The man is not stupid.

This *criollo* is a middle class specimen and holds a personal view of what are Puerto Rico and its problems. It would be equally foolish to think that this man is unique. Others, many, who live as he does think as he does. They have a petit-bourgeois view and understanding of Puerto Rico and its problems. He and many others like him—though hesitantly—once in a while, and sometimes strongly, defends the country's independence. His interest in it is of his own class interest. But this interest does not in any way diminish his indisputable patriotic feelings.

Let us move on to a household that represents the majority of the population. The sixty-nine percent [60] that inhabit the countryside. We climb the highlands of Puerto Rico. Dawn is beginning. Wrapped in shadows we see a hut. A man has just gulped down a mouthful of hot black coffee, he half opened the door and jumped outside onto the front yard of his humble dwelling. He goes into the rainy dawn without a raincoat or sweater, dressed only with a shirt and pants, and a tattered straw hat. He feels the cold rain on his bones. His bare feet sink into the mud. He will work that way all day, and return at to the hut at sundown to partake of a frugal meal.

---

60 Congressional Record, Volume 33, Part 3, Page 2649, quoted by Mejías in his work: *Condiciones de vida de las clases jornaleras.*

There are thousands like him. Around 2,000 [61] families live that way. They are the lowest stratum of Puerto Rican society. They are neither learned nor moneyed, nor of brilliant speeches, and have been the victims of triple slavery: imperialism, national oppression, and class yoke. With their many children and working hands, they represent the greater numbers of nationhood, and together with the workers from the towns and cities, they make up the largest patriotic front for the defense of independence. In their hands rests, indisputably, our future. It is for them that independence has a wider and more profound meaning.

Who would think that those men and women might have a vision, an understanding of Puerto Rico and its problems, just as does the self-satisfied bourgeois from Villa Caparra and the comfortable businessman from outside the metropolitan area? Of course, the workers' viewpoints and understandings of Puerto Rico and its problems are not the same as the others'. Their viewpoint is a working class viewpoint.

Among these classes of Puerto Ricans there are necessarily contradictory interests. That cannot be denied. Clearly, imperial politics has not forgotten them. Support, as the circumstances arise, one class against the other, has accomplished separation between them, or has brought them together at its convenience. Such as during the two great crises of imperialism that caused the two past world wars.63 That is to be expected.

It is us the patriots who have been foolish. The independence movement has never endeavored to produce a coincidence of all the class interests, necessary for national unity and the conquest of a common goal: independence. Neither the party of the bourgeoisie when that class had one that favored independence, nor the petit-bourgeois parties for independence, nor the workers' parties have put forth a correct political line for the achievement of national unity in order to agglutinate the great masses of workers and peasants around the need the fight for liberation.

There are two predominant petit-bourgeois schools of thought in the independence movement. Let us look at what they say about the masses. One states that the great masses are neutral. Too heavy to be moved with the needed speed toward the filth for independence.

---

61 Op. cit.

Weighed down by a weak national consciousness it is not prepared to play an active role in the great drama of our emancipation. It is necessary, then, to liberate it from bondage. With lack of self-interest, the noble patriotic effort of sacrificing one self for it must be realized, so that it moves unwittingly from slavery to freedom through the effective and vicarious actions of the minority and glorious chorus made up by the initiated, the heroes, the martyrs. With this naive good faith, based on this probably pure and patriotic intention beats the heart of the typically impatient petit-bourgeoisie.

History has proven, however, that for a nation to achieve freedom, the idea of independence has to win the hearts and minds of the working and peasant masses.

The independence of South America consolidated when, in Venezuela—where two republics have risen and fallen—José Antonio Páez joined Bolívar's genius with the peasant forces that had been at the command of the bloodthirsty royalist Boves.

Cuba became independent from Spain when a son of the Spanish working class—who became a lawyer but did not forget to "cast his lot with the poor people of the Earth"—José Martí, transfigured his genius for organization and his task of organizing in apostolate and, when the "heroic Blacks" move from the ranks to the leadership of the War for Independence and the tobacco workers poured their wages into financing the revolutionary forces, saving the day for Cuba after the tragic events of La Fernandina. [62] In the face of that example, we the Puerto Ricans cannot but painfully remember what we have not been able to accomplish.

The second petit-bourgeois school of thought is expressed at a lower level. For to its acolytes the great masses of Puerto Rico lack national consciousness, are ignorant, servile and without awareness. And those factors prevent any revolutionary proposal for the Puerto Rican problem. They must be "educated". They have to be told that they are aware, intelligent and proud, and can become free from the imperialist yoke by voting for independence in imperialism's elections. And when it happens

---

62 Estate where the Spanish Government seized weapons and executed Cuban independentists, in 1892.

that, "It takes one to know one," that the masses do not vote, then the chorus of mourners is heard loudly: "The people are ingrates! They are servile!" And turn to the revolutionaries with the attitude of disappointed know-it-alls and say: "Didn't we tell you? With these people we can't get ahead! They are a bunch of degenerates!"

These fools forget that we are all part of the same populace. Unless they, sublime specimens, were begotten by the Holy Spirit, in a predestined womb! They also forget a tremendously important detail: nothing, absolutely nothing can take the place of experience in the revolutionary struggle to educate the masses.

This failure of the independence movement to elicit the inclusion of the country's masses of workers and peasants is based on the reality that Puerto Rican society is made up by classes who behave politically by forming diverse political parties. Therefore, the fight for Puerto Rican independence has been led by, at best, a petit-bourgeois party, or at worst, as in the present, by two parties of the petit-bourgeoisie who reflect that class's two sectors, each one reflecting its own resplendent view of the ever present petit-bourgeois illusions who swear and guarantee that national unity is achievable within one single party. Thus, they disregard the historical experience of countries that have enjoyed independence for a long time, and are suddenly attacked by a foreign enemy. The national unity in defense of its threatened independence cannot be achieved by only one party, which points to the deeper truth that national unity in a country subjected to colonialism is much less likely to occur within a single party.

Scientific analysis of our problem dismisses that illusion, and points unequivocally to the right organizational path that our nation must take to be free. Puerto Rico needs a new tool for independence. It cannot be a political party, but a united front against imperialism. The formation of the front does not presuppose the extinction of the existing political parties, nor the abolition of class struggle, nor the classes giving up their particular interests. It presupposes the understanding, in patriotic terms, and the necessary frame of mind to comprehend that independence will be an accomplished fact only when we have dispelled the worst of our sins: disunity. Independence is a national goal—not a party interest—that will benefit all Puerto Ricans.

By its own diverse nature, a united front against imperialism cannot respond to the desires of just one class. But it can unite all of the present patriotic camps, bring to the struggle wider groups of society, definitely incorporate the workers and peasants to the active fight for independence, and consolidate national unity which would guarantee the attainment of independence.

A united people are strong! A united people are invincible!

14

THE IDEALS OF NATIONHOOD

Throughout this work we have put forth the thesis that Puerto Rico was not liberated from Spain in the [nineteenth century] [63] because the liberal-reformists weakened the revolutionary forces, leaving the country with low defenses and offenses at the mercy of the foreign dominator. We have also stated that the Island has not freed itself from United States imperialism because the same liberal-reformism survived into the twentieth century and has manacled the country and surrendered it to the insanity, abjection and exploitation on the part of the United States. This does not mean that at either instance Puerto Rico lacked the forces to liberate them, but that they were, in every instance, betrayed.

And we have proven that the services of liberal-reformism to two empires have been against the happiness, plenitude, progress and independence of our Homeland and have been successful thanks to a malicious and criminal adulteration of the ideals of the Puerto Rican nationhood. This downgrading has been employed to deceive the people and make them pursue a mirage of its true ideals, in such a manner that believing to be striving for the basic ideals rooted in their needs, they have really rushed unto the precipice of abject and degrading colonialism.

Undoubtedly, Puerto Rico has sufficient forces to become free from Yankee imperialism. It has the strengths to become independent by forcing and vanquishing the empire's will to enslave us, and the forces to destroy all of the imperialist-colonial machinery. The empire seeks to destroy Puerto Rican nationhood, because it is necessary for its definitive domination over Puerto Rico.

The purpose of the independence movement is to salvage our people through organization, so that they realize fully their historical destiny.

---

63 Translator's change from "…last century…" in original text.

Therefore, the total destruction of the imperialist-colonial regime is a necessity for the triumph of independence.

The People's Assembly for the Republic would be the instrument with sufficient strength to destroy the [present] regime totally. It would also have enough creative energy to produce the institutions that Puerto Rico needs to be saved and realize its historic destiny to the fullest.

The malicious perversion of the ideals of Puerto Rican nationhood we mentioned is blocking the revolutionary way today as it did in the past. Here is, then, the explanation as to which are the true ideals of Puerto Rican nationhood.

The first ideal is its endurance. It presupposes the survival and at the same time constant development of national characteristics, subject to change, as is every historic phenomenon. A healthy and logical interpretation of a country's people exposure to historical change does not assume the destruction of their characteristics, but their constant improvement.

Deceived by liberal-reformism, following their natural ideal of endurance in history, but subject to the law of change, the people of Puerto Rico, have been led blindly towards assimilation; first with Spain, and later with the United States. This means the destruction of the possibilities for historical survival.

The second ideal is drawn from the premise that the Puerto Rican nation is a stable community that formed historically. So the natural ideal of the people is to reach the plenitude of their historical development as consequence of the constant growth and progress of their natural formation.

Deceived by liberal-reformism, instead of taking the route that the revolutionary forces offer, the Puerto Rican people have been detoured into confusing their history, first with Spanish history, and later with United States history which is equivalent to embarking on the destruction of the fulfillment of its own historical destiny.

When Puerto Rico formed historically, the language in common for its people became Spanish. The United States imposed English as the official language. [64] The task of liberal-reformists has been to prevent

---

64 Presently, English and Spanish are official languages.

independence and with that maintained such confusing conditions that the language of the islanders may be lost.

In having a common language of their own, it is natural that Puerto Ricans use it in their literature in such an exalted manner that Puerto Rican literature shall be a tool with which the people would collaborate with the other peoples of the world to raise the human spirit as never before. In retaining the United States invader on Puerto Rican soil, liberal-reformists prevent the people of Puerto Rico from realizing that ideal which the revolutionary forces call for.

To be a nation, to grow and take shape, Puerto Rico needs, of course, its own territory. That it has. The Island's natural boundaries are its political frontiers. And because of our advantageous island condition, our coasts and territorial waters are precise and undeniable. Only bad faith, greed, larceny, piracy, or treason can attempt at breaking them up.

Puerto Rican territory belongs to the Puerto Ricans. Yet, we have seen how in [almost a century] [65] the collaboration of the liberal-reformists with the invader has propitiated the total domination of the Homeland by the government of the United States; and how the monopolies and expanding militarism of that country have fragmented our national territory. In order to give national lands to the armed forces of the United States, the liberal-reformists invented a new trick: to speak of dividing the lands of the monopolies among the peasants. But meanwhile, quietly and secretly, they increasingly surrender our best lands to the United States military forces. With this, the liberal-reformists stand in the way of another ideal: the lawful possession and enjoyment of our natural resources.

This automatically frustrated another ideal of nationhood: to generate a normal and healthy system of economic relations among Puerto Ricans, which can only be based on the exploitation of Puerto Rican lands and industries so that the islanders consume the products of their lands and their industries. The frustration of that ideal cannot be taken lightly, because the economy is the basis of Nationhood.

The frustration of all the necessary ideals carries the frustration of yet another great ideal: The future of the culture. Our culture is destined to

---

65 Translator's change from original text that says "…half a century…"

serve universal culture by contributing to the universal development of the multinational cultural nucleus that comprises our linguistic family: The Hispanic family of nations. What kind of future does liberal-reformism at the service of United States imperialism pretend to assign us? None other than to serve as a bridge to penetrate the Hispanic countries of America with the power of their militaristic monopolies to seize their riches and ultimately destroy them. Essentially, the future that they want for Puerto Rican culture is to be incentive and example for the total degradation and slavery for *Hispanoamérica*. In contrast, the Puerto Rican revolutionary forces want to guide the people to take its cultural position in the world, and become a part of universal culture to enrich the cultural pool of its linguistic family, the Hispanic family of nations.

A theory of political ideals has grown from the nature of Puerto Rican nationhood by virtue of its condition as Hispanoamerican nation. It can be divided in two groups and which we shall designate as the ideals of the founders of our Homeland and the ideals of Bolívar. The two groups are inseparable from each other. They make up and give substance to our national and international policies. (When I say "our" I mean our people, equivalent to the revolutionary forces who will guide the country to salvation and realization.)

What are the ideals of Betances and Hostos, and of the Puerto Ricans who were on their side during their long and glorious apostolate? First and foremost, the immediate independence for Puerto Rico. For Betances and Hostos the right of Puerto Rico to independence was essential and indisputable from the practical point of view; just as it was indisputable its immediacy. For both men any delay of independence was a crime and a betrayal.

In light of the thought of Betances and Hostos regarding the ideals of Puerto Rican nationhood, any external force that opposes the immediate independence of Puerto Rico is criminal, and any opposing internal force is treasonous; and all foreigners and nationals who oppose immediate independence for Puerto Rico are traitors and criminals.

Betances and Hostos, and the rest of the patricians, loved and respected the people, had faith in them, and were inspired by them to fight for independence. There are no liberators without love, respect, and faith in the people. That is why both wanted that what guided the

Puerto Rican people to organize for independence, including the highest form of progress. Consequently, they wanted to read the past from the point of view of the future. It is an ideal of the Puerto Ricans, made sublime by its most illustrious sons, to illuminate the road to independence and its organization with progress. And the spirits of Betances and Hostos would curse, not only those opposing the immediate organization for the independence of Puerto Rico, but any one who opposes that the organization of our independence be done and turned into reality with the shining lights of progress and the most advanced thinking in every respect.

Our people have as well been detoured regarding the ideal of progress. The liberal-reformists who serve United States imperialism distorted it. Specially now, with the pack led by Puppet Luis Muñoz Marín. He and his followers present the country wrapped in progress, but under the wrapping is none other than colonialism, slavery, servility, collaborationism, political blackmail and international degradation.

The idea of an Antillean Federation originated with Betances. Hostos became his apostle, searched and pinned his hopes on the idea, and both fought intensely to realize it. Both men agreed that Puerto Rico needed to be independent before the federation was organized. "Without a free Puerto Rico," he wrote to Morales Lemus, [66] "Federation is impossible." For both, America was incomplete if Puerto Rico was not free, and the world was unfinished and unbalanced without a united Latin America and a federated Antilles. They were true followers of Bolívar's belief that Latin America should be united. And they coincided in the belief that the Antillean Federation and its organization be guided by progressive political thought. Hostos wrote: "...the Antilles must be organized democratically until they can attain a socially more advanced form of government."

Our ideal is independence for Puerto Rico and the Antillean Federation. When we fight for independence, we also fight for the

---

66 José Morales Lemus was a Cuban lawyer and businessman who professed moderate liberal ideas. He disliked Spanish domination, and for a time favored Cuba's annexation to the United States. However, after the U.S. Civil War made this impossible, he joined the reformists, a group of prominent *criollos* who advocated constitutional reforms within the framework of Spanish rule.

Antillean Federation and Latin American unity. But we know, because we have read it and have suffered it, that for the Antilles to federate, Latin America to unite, and for America and the world to be complete; so that the Antilles may organize truly democratically and later may be organized "a government socially more advanced," it is necessary to fight, courageously, in a revolutionary manner, for Puerto Rican independence. But the struggle for independence must be understood and conducted as anti-imperialist, as part of the fight waged by all anti-imperialists of the Antilles and the world. We know that to securely convert Puerto Rican independence into absolute national security so that it may serve the people without limitations to pursue happiness and functioning within the Antillean Federation. It is also absolutely necessary for Latin American unity become a reality, the total destruction of United States Imperialism. That is, the United States government as we know it, must disappear for the good of all our peoples and also for the good of the people of the United States. It is an essential duty of our generation to become an actor in its disappearance.

This notion of coordinating the universal anti-imperialist forces to fight imperialism is also ours, absolutely and legitimately ours. We have found it and imbibed it in the never ending fountain of he of whose sword "gave us life": Simón Bolívar, *El Libertador* [The Liberator]. What we do now is to emphasize his presence in our struggle.

In effect, one hundred eighty-six years ago, yes! One hundred eighty-six years have passed since December 31, 1813, "Very early in his career, a thirty-year-old man, in the midst of the hardships of the terrible Venezuelan war, Bolívar had his Minister of State publish a very important and transcendental document. No one, until now, has pointed out its importance. It appeared in the thirtieth volume of *La gaceta de Caracas*. It reveals the magnitude of Bolívar's internationalist political thought." [67] Here is what he says in that extraordinary and revealing writing:

"After the continental balance sought by Europe where it seems the least to be found-in the midst of war and agitation-there is another equilibrium, the one that matters to us: the balance of the Universe. The

---

67 Rufino Blanco Fombona, *El pensamiento vivo de Bolívar.*

ambition of Europe's nations leads the other parts of the world to slavery. All of those parts of the world should try to strike a balance between themselves and Europe to destroy its dominance. This is what I call the balance of the Universe and it must enter into political calculations." [68] Years later (1826), he wanted to take freedom to the Far East, the Philippines; and he wants to fight, not only on the side of Asia against European ambitions, but he dared to seek the beast in its lair. Ships bearing the Colombian flag took on the perilous mission of threatening the Andalusian coast at the Mediterranean. French diplomats were in an uproar, they alerted Spain, and through their ambassador in Madrid expressed the fear that if Hispanoamerican republican troops approached, the Spanish revolutionaries would seek support from them. So it was, in effect, a real possibility." [69]

That was Bolívar's plan. His endeavors regarding the Antilles were described by Emeterio S. Santovenia in *Bolívar y las Antillas hispanas*. He planned also to liberate Cuba and Puerto Rico. From Puerto Rico travel to Spain and, with the cooperation of the Spanish people, topple the monarchy and establish a republic. In preparation, he made an exploratory voyage to our Isle of Vieques. [70]

Today, [one hundred and eighty-six] years after that brilliant document was written by Bolívar, Puerto Rico is not yet free, the Antilles have not become a federation, nor Latin America has united. Today, of the [six billion] [71] human beings who inhabit the earth, [72] live in abject poverty. They are the inhabitants of the colonies, semi-colonies and dependent nations, ourselves included, of Latin America, Africa and Asia. [73] And today, it is not a European country-as it was in Bolívar's lifetime-although there are European countries who are imperialist centers, but the United States, the power that with its atomic-imperialism heads the oligarchy of imperialist nations that own and exploit the colonial nations, despotically.

---

68 José Félix Blanco y Ramón Azpurúa, *Documentos para la historia del Libertador*, 1813.

69 Rufino Blanco Fombona, *El pensamiento vivo de Bolívar*.

70 Perea, *Bolívar en Puerto Rico*, "El Mundo", 1930.

71 Translator's demographic update to 1999.

72 Translator's demographic update to 1999.

73 Kumar Goshal, *People in the Colonies*.

Therefore, that union of colonial nations against the imperialist powers that Bolívar dreamed of is still needed. It is our plan for struggle against imperialism and, in particular, against United States imperialism. Bolívar's incomparable genius foresaw who our present enemy would be when he stated that "the United States seem to have placed itself as an obstacle to the freedom of the American peoples." [74] It was he who also intercepted the incipient "Pan Americanism" by calling the Latin American nations to the *Conferencia Anfictiónica del Istmo* (Amphyctionic Conference at the Isthmus).[75]

At the request of the Libertador, Santander invited the American Nations to the *Congreso Internacional de Panamá*. He failed in his charge and invited England, Holland and the United States. Did Santander not understand the transcendence of Bolívar's plan? That cannot be assumed, as El Libertador's letters to Santander demonstrate that Bolívar trusted him. [76]

It is common knowledge that Bolívar was against inviting the United States to the Isthmus meeting.

If three-fourths of humanity—three-fourths who inhabit the planet live in miserable conditions in the colonies, victims of international imperialism, not only they-that is, us-are their victims. Billions of human beings live in bondage, abject poverty and misery, within the imperialist countries. For example, the blacks and poor whites of the southern states of the United States. In other instances, the struggle [for hegemony] among the imperialists themselves adds heaps tragedy over the power's own poorest citizens.

The people of England suffer hunger and cold under the despotism of the English oligarchy. And that hunger and cold that they are forced to endure is increased to the point of horror by the added pressure from the competition with their brotherly cousins, the United States monopolies.

---

74 Isidro Fabela, *Estados Unidos contra la libertad.*
75 Conference of delegates of the Hispanoamerican Independent Nations, called by Bolívar with the intention of forming a Latin American union, held in that part of the Central American Isthmus where Panamá is today.
76 Rufino Blanco Fombona, *El pensamiento vivo de Bolívar.*

Bolívar wanted to gain the allegiance of the Spanish people and launch them to revolt against Spanish monarchy. What he attempted early in the nineteenth century Betances tried at the end. We will follow suit by encouraging and aiding the people of the United States to rise against their government. This is the only appropriate approach that we the Puerto Ricans can offer the people of the United States. And also the only approach that the rest of Hispanoamerica can offer. All else has been and continues to be surrender, cowardice and treason, regardless of how it is disguised.

Using as a point of departure their own bitter experiences, the Puerto Rican people now regroup revolutionary forces. They will march fearlessly towards freedom. Independence will turn its back on the reformist traitors who have spoken deafeningly in favor of [United States colonialism] and who continue do so as followers of the Partido Popular [and the pro-statehood party, the *Partido Nuevo Progresista*] [77]. It will also turn its back on those who want to put a stop to and frustrate [the process of independence] by steering them to the electioneering camp, and on the pseudo intellectuals who lack revolutionary spine, on the cowards of the mind, on the dialectic of "putting up with," and on the balloteering doctorate. There is no time or room for stopping and talking to the professionals of debate. Our hands are full with mounds of work, it fills our thoughts, makes our tongue economize energy on words. We must speak only when necessary and work beyond our strength.

This is the way to set our Homeland on the way to revolution; the only path-so that we may fulfill the magnificent ideals of our nationhood by conquering and helping our America and all the peoples on this earth to attain the highest degree possible of freedom within a complete independence and an ever improving form of liberty!

---

77 Translator's note: Pro-annexation party, governing in 1999.

15

THE TASK AHEAD

In 1810, Hispanic America began the great endeavor of attaining independence. It seemed that the task would be completed once the flag of the monarchy residing in Madrid was lowered from all of the posts in America. But there is still much work to be done.

Eighty-eight years later the last Spanish flag in America was lowered in Puerto Rico. This gave closure to four centuries of drama for the world Hispanics. However, it also has another meaning. It proved that those who thought that the lowering of the Spanish flag meant the completion of the struggle for independence in Hispanic America had not seen their wish for freedom satisfied nor its promise fulfilled. But they knew the significance of the nineteenth century in America.

That meaning promptly became very clear in the minds of the Hispanoamericans of the time and we answered the call quickly and eagerly. It meant political separation from Spain, the substitution of the monarchic institutions for republican ones, the subversion of feudalism, and taking the road toward industry, technology, capitalism and democracy.

This is the true significance of the Hispanoamerican nineteenth century. Moved by this task, Spain should also awake from its monarchic sleep. With our example and assistance, the Spanish people should replace monarchic institutions for republican ones, subvert feudalism and take the road to industry, technology, capitalism and democracy. Taking the cue from Bolívar's plan of a unified Hispanic America under a common political thought, made up by great multinational states, Spain should find solutions to the problems of the nations within the Iberian Peninsula.

The response to the call to arms for liberation was prompt and eager. But in the dizzying race towards progress the sight of the goal was lost. Anarchy and reaction captured the heart of the Hispanoamerican Revolution and it went backward. The disaster began with the

displacement of Mariano Moreno [78] and the triumph of the reactionary
clique that gathered in the *Logia Lautaro* (Lautaro Masonic Lodge). [79] It
worsened when the great chief of the Uruguayan peasants, José Artigas [80]
was incarcerated in Paraguay, and took on disastrous proportions when
Antonio José Sucre [81] was assassinated. Nevertheless, Bolívar did not plow
on water. His work is the pedestal of our future.

Through the process of disintegration enough colonial elements were
revived in our republics to thwart the full realization of independence.
The pounds sterling, the franks and the dollars entered trough the doors
opened by the dead heroes. That penetration is what has given the twentieth century its Hispanoamerican significance. In 1898 the flag of United
States imperialism replaced the monarchic flag of Spain in Puerto Rico.
From that moment on the soon to be born twentieth century acquired
a deeply Puerto Rican Hispanoamerican meaning, because the ousting
of Imperialism from all Hispanoamerican lands, will begin in Puerto
Rico. There is a need for a new war of Latin American independence
against United States imperialism, more urgent and far reaching than the
one fought in the nineteenth century. And in that war Puerto Rico will
be the last battleground backward and the first forward.

Perhaps there are not too many thinking people in the world who can
comprehend or grasp intuitively the importance of a Puerto Rico actively
involved in revolutionary struggle against the United States. It would be
an example for the rest of Latin America and the world. Our great love
for our Homeland has given heart to thousands of Puerto Ricans. And
for us, the pressing historical task of liberating our country, the immediate
attainment of independence raises it to a Hispanoamerican dimension

---

78 Mariano Moreno was an Argentinean patriot who was Secretary of the Junta
    Revolucionaria in Buenos Aires in 1810. He was forced to resign because of his
    disagreements with the Junta's powerful president.
79 The powerful Argentinean right wing conspirators who plotted to take over the
    government were members of the Lautaro Masonic Lodge.
80 José Gervasio Artigas was founding father of Uruguay. He fought for indepen-
    dence from Spain and from Argentina.
81 Antonio José de Sucre was a Venezuelan who fought alongside Bolívar for the in-
    dependence of Hispanoamerica from Spain. He commanded the winning forces
    that defeated the Viceroy in the Battle of Ayacucho, a decisive event in ousting
    Spain from the American continent.

and through that to a world dimension. The magnitude of our work, which is the exclusive Puerto Rican job of starting the fire in Latin America against the empire; of turning the Island into an incendiary bomb that sets fires against United States imperialism throughout our continent.

Puerto Rican reformists of all shades, absolutely all who preach absurd and suicidal "law and order," concurrence to the polls; all those who preach and constrain their activities to the exclusive use of legalistic means are contributing to slow down—but only that, because they will not be able to stop it—the revolutionary process that will spark the new Hispanoamerican war of independence.

Very soon most of them, through conviction or repentance, will join the revolutionary forces. History will find the rest hiding under their beds, where they will join Luis Muñoz Marín.

AFTERWORD TO THE FIRST ENGLISH EDITION

By Oscar López Rivera

In 1999, fourteen years after Don Juan Antonio Corretjer's death and fifty after the publication of his seminal book: "The Struggle for the Independence of Puerto Rico" the Independence Movement came together and, for four years, it struggled and worked day and night until it forced the US government to close its naval base and stop operations in Vieques. It was a tremendous victory and achievement, because it had resolved one of the most destructive and deleterious problems the people of that island municipality had been experiencing for decades. Unfortunately, the Independence Movement failed to appreciate and internalize the fact that such a victory had been achieved because it had struggled and worked together. Rather than daring to organize a United Front to continue waging the necessary struggle to end colonial domination in Puerto Rico and secure independence and sovereignty for our beloved homeland, it chose to go back to its previous *modus operandi*.

The visionary and revolutionary idea of organizing a solid united front had been proposed by Don Juan Antonio Corretjer five decades earlier. According to him it was the necessary and fundamental step the Independence Movement had to take to achieve victory and overcome the unproductive and opportunistic practice of the reformist tendency that had plagued it since its beginnings. Instead of working to create the United Front, the reformist tendency chose to participate in the 2004 colonial elections (for the fourteenth time since the publication of Don Juan's book), only one year after the momentous victory in Vieques.

The elections were not only a disaster for the reformist tendency—because the Puerto Rican Independence Party lost its franchise—but also ended up being a disgraceful and damaging spectacle for the Movement and for the Puerto Rican people. Participation in the colonial elections continues to be a destructive fiasco Don Juan had averred that such a practice would be, five decades earlier. And to complicate and make matters worse for the whole Independence Movement, this nefarious practice has become the Independence Movement's Reformist Tendency's main strategy for seeking Puerto Rico's independence. What should be used only as a tactic has become the main strategy, thus making it impossible for the Revolutionary Tendency to use the badly needed tactic of boycotting colonial elections.

After reading the book, it begs the question why the independence movement failed to heed his recommendations or pay attention to his analysis. The book presents a clear and succinct analysis of the struggle for independence and provides feasible and viable ideas and solutions. Yet it seems the Independence Movement prefers to remain mired in a limbo where the Reformist Tendency can continue undoing or undermining the work carried out by the Revolutionary Tendency.

Let's hope the book's English translation becomes an inspirational tool for the new generation of independentists. It's the new generation that can best emulate Don Juan's revolutionary example. The book reflects and depicts his genius and the revolutionary life he lived. To emulate his example is to live a life full of love, hope and courage, which are the basic elements necessary to face and deal with any challenge the struggle presents. Dare to read the book and to share it with others! Dare to appreciate the great potential we have if we choose to unite in one solid front! Dare to meld your new and fresh ideas with his, to give impetus to the struggle and achieve victory! Dare to struggle, dare to win! And bear in mind: it will take a REVOLUTION to achieve Puerto Rico's independence and sovereignty. UNITED WE CAN'T BE DEFEATED. Long live *Comandante* Juan Antonio Corretjer's revolutionary example!

Oscar López Rivera is [82] served 37 of a 70-year sentence for his commitment to the estruggle for Puerto Rican independence. Carlos Alberto Torres, who was sentenced to 78 years of imprisonment, along with Oscar López Rivera, and endured 30 years of imprisonment.

---

82 Editor's Note: Carlos Alberto Torres was released from prison on July 26, 2010; Oscar López Rivera, on May 17, 2017.

AFTERWORD TO THE SECOND ENGLISH EDITION

By Consuelo Corretjer Lee

Using as a point of departure their own bitter experiences, the Puerto Rican people must now regroup revolutionary forces. They must march fearlessly towards freedom. Independence will turn its back on the reformist traitors and the followers of the *Partido Popular* and pro-statehood party, the *Partido Nuevo Progresista* [83]. who advocate deafeningly in favor of United States colonialism. It will also turn its back on those who want to frustrate independence by steering them to the electioneering camp, and on the pseudo intellectuals who lack revolutionary spine, on the cowards of the mind, on "putting up with," and on the balloteering doctorate. There is no time or room for stopping and talking to the professionals of debate. Our hands are full with mounds of work, it fills our thoughts, we must economize energy on words. We must speak only when necessary and work beyond our strength.

This is the way to set our Homeland on the way to revolution; the only path so that we may fulfill the magnificent ideals of our Nationhood by conquering and helping Our America and all the peoples on this earth to attain the highest degree possible of freedom within a complete independence and an ever improving form of liberty!

---

83 Pro-annexation party governing in 2020.

BIOGRAPHY OF JUAN ANTONIO CORRETJER

(MARCH 3, 1908 – JANUARY 19, 1985)

Juan Antonio Corretjer, born in Ciales, Puerto Rico on March 3, 1908, was a poet of extraordinary sensibility, essayist, journalist, and gifted speaker. One of the most important Puerto Rican political and literary figures of all time, his many poetic works were inspired by his love for his homeland. Life in the country is presented in all of its dimensions and perspectives, gathering the innermost feelings of the nation, and shaping the poetic lifeblood of its history. A recurrent theme in his poetry is the love of family, which to him is not only parents, wife, and children, but also the people from his country.

Corretjer the writer of prose has a collection of short stories, *El cumplido*, and an important collection of essays, that probe into the very heart of Puerto Rico's historical problems, and the contradictions between the reformist and revolutionary tendencies that have characterized the struggle for national liberty. His works about literary and patriotic figures, the function and meaning of art, the imperial colonial impositions on the Puerto Ricans, and the myths, realities and future of the Island combine a deep knowledge of his country and of the writer's craft.

In 1924 the magazine *Puerto Rico Ilustrado* published some of his early poems, and in 1927 he was initiated into journalism at the newspaper *La Democracia*, where he worked as a reporter, writer, editorialist and columnist, totally immersed in a literary career.

But his course changed in 1930, when he joined the *Partido Nacionalista* (Nationalist Party) and was elected secretary, as Pedro Albizu Campos became president. He participated in the assault to the colonial senate in 1932, and in the sugar industry workers' strike of 1934. That year he was appointed the party's delegate abroad to obtain support for the cause of independence. He traveled to the Dominican Republic, Haiti, and Cuba, participated in the Cuban general strike of March 1935, was arrested, imprisoned, tried, declared *persona non grata*, and expelled from that country.

A year after returning from Cuba, he was jailed at La Princesa for refusing to surrender the minutes and log books of the *Partido Nacionalista* to the Federal Court. On July 30, 1936, he received a ten-year sentence of imprisonment and exile with Albizu Campos, Luis F. Velázquez, Clemente Soto Vélez, Erasmo Velázquez, Pablo Rosado Ortiz, Juan Gallardo Santiago, and Julio Héctor Velázquez. All were transported to a federal prison in Atlanta, Georgia on June 7, 1937.

In addition to his journalistic career in Puerto Rico, Corretjer worked in that profession in Cuba and the United States. He founded several newspapers of pro independence editorial line in Puerto Rico, directed the *Partido Nacionalista*'s newspaper, *El Nacionalista*, and founded and directed *Pueblos Hispanos*, while in exile in New York from 1943 until 1945. Returned from exile, Corretjer continued his political activism through organizing, public speaking and writing against United States Imperialism in Puerto Rico until the end of his life.

He was Night Editor for *El Imparcial*, and later, opinion page writer and reporter for *El Mundo*. When the Cuban Revolution triumphed he was assigned to report from Havana about the newborn revolution. He was also guest writer for *El Nuevo Día* during his later years.

Corretjer was a gifted speaker whose style was influenced by José de Diego and Pedro Albizu Campos. During the decade of 1930, he took part in the struggles led by the *Partido Nacionalista* (Nationalist Party), and helped carve nationalism's place in the history of Puerto Rico. His oratory, modern in content and ideology was passionate and deep, precise, and clear. His Marxist orientation called for revolutionary mobilization of the masses. The rights of Puerto Rico to independence, and of the working class to total participation in the island's economic and political life were ever present in his speeches and writings.

Corretjer's influence on art and politics are notable. When still an adolescent, he helped found in his hometown an Independentist group: *Sociedad Literaria José Gautier Benítez*, and was a member of the *Juventud Nacionalista* (Nationalist Youth). In 1924, he and a fellow student were expelled from Horace Mann School in Ciales, for organizing a strike demanding that classes not be given during *Semana Santa* (Holy Week) and that the school's name be changed to José de Diego.

Between 1948 and 1964, Corretjer organized several Independentist groups. The *Liga Socialista Puertorriqueña* was the last one, which he led as Secretary General until his death on January 19, 1985.

When the 1950 Nationalist Uprising took place, Corretjer was falsely accused and imprisoned for incitement to riot. In 1969, together with other *Liga Socialista* members—including his wife Consuelo Lee Tapia and patriot Carmín Pérez—was arrested, and accused of conspiracy. The legal battles lasted until 1971 when he went to El Castillo prison in Ponce, and Consuelo and Carmín were sent to the Cárcel de Mujeres in Vega Alta. Finally, all were finally exonerated of all charges and released.

The Puerto Rican communities in the United States knew him as the voice for surviving *puertorriqueñidad* (Puertoricanness) despite the up rootedness and exile. Corretjer was always present where there was a struggle for the rights of his people, and unwavering faith in justice for all peoples was his trademark.

OTHER WORKS BY JUAN ANTONIO CORRETJER

Poetry

Agüeybana, Ulises, Amor de Puerto Rico, Cántico de guerra, El leñero, Los primeros años, Tierra nativa, Alabanza en la Torre de Ciales, Don Diego en El Cariño, Distancias, Un recuerdo de Cuba, Genio y figura (rapsodia criolla), Un viaje en cucubano, Quieto en mi isla voy, Yerba bruja, Pausa para el amor, Canciones de Consuelo que son canciones de protesta, Construcción del sur, Aguinaldo escarlata, Paso a Venezuela, Para que los pueblos canten, La noche de San Pedro, El estado del tiempo, Los días contados

Drama

Los siete compañeros, play written in poetic form about the Lares Uprising of 1868, and the Jayuya Uprising of 1950.

Short stories

El cumplido

Essays

El buen borincano, Llorens, juicio histórico, La revolución de Lares, Nuestra bandera, La lucha por la independencia de Puerto Rico, Contestación al miedo, La patria radical, Futuro sin falla, Hostos y Albizu Campos, Albizu Campos and the Ponce Massacre, Albizu Campos hombre histórico, Albizu Campos y las huelgas en los años 30, La sangre en huelga, El espíritu de Lares,

La historia que gritó en Lares, Mitología del Grito de Lares, Lares y Jayuya, Y después de Jayuya, ¿qué?, Vieques y la lucha por la independencia, Problemas de la guerra popular en Puerto Rico, La gloria de Don Pedro Angleró (in *Plantao en la revolución*, by Don Pedro Angleró), *Homenaje al compañero Ángel Rodríguez Cristobal, El líder de la desesperación, Fusilamiento en "Maravilla"* (about the 1978 entrapment and killing of two independentist youths), *Poesía y revolución* (essays about culture, edited by Joserramón Meléndes), *Puerto Rico: pueblo invencible* (last speech given on November 30, 1984).

Journalism

Directed and wrote for: "El Nacionalista", newspaper of the Partido Nacionalista de Puerto Rico.

Founded, directed and wrote for: "Pueblos Hispanos" (New York), La palabra, "¡Adelante!", "Prieto y puya", "Bandera", "Pabellón", "El boricua", "Unión del Pueblo pro Constituyente", "Correo de la quincena", "El socialista" (all in Puerto Rico).

Wrote for: "Puerto Rico Ilustrado", "El Imparcial", and "El Mundo"

Was a guest writer for "El Nuevo Día" (Puerto Rico), "Daily Worker" (New York), "Hoy" (Cuba).